Export Strategies

Export Strategies

Navigating International Markets

Maria M

Modern Publishing

CONTENTS

INDEX 1

Chapter 1 3

Chapter 2 20

Chapter 3 36

Chapter 4 54

Chapter 5 72

Chapter 6 89

Chapter 7 109

Chapter 8 126

Chapter 9 141

INDEX

Chapter 1: Introduction
1.1 Brief overview of the importance of international markets for businesses
1.2 Key reasons for adopting export strategies
1.3 Challenges and opportunities in global trade

Chapter 2: Understanding International Markets
2.1 Analysis of different international markets and their dynamics
2.2 Cultural, economic, and political factors affecting market entry
2.3 Identification of potential target markets

Chapter 3: Market Research and Analysis
3.1 Importance of thorough market research before entering a new market
3.2 Tools and methodologies for market analysis
3.3 Studies illustrating successful and unsuccessful market entries

Chapter 4: Developing a Robust Export Plan
4.1 Crafting a comprehensive export plan
4.2 Setting clear objectives and goals for international expansion
4.3 Strategies for product adaptation and customization

Chapter 5: Legal and Regulatory Considerations
5.1 Overview of international trade laws and regulations
5.2 Compliance requirements for exporting goods and services
5.3 Mitigating legal risks in foreign markets

Chapter 6: Building Strategic Partnerships
6.1 Importance of forming alliances with local partners
6.2 Types of strategic partnerships: joint ventures, distributorships, licensing

6.3 Showcasing successful collaboration models

Chapter 7: Logistics and Supply Chain Management
7.1 Efficient supply chain management in international trade
7.2 Transportation modes and logistics considerations
7.3 Warehouse management and inventory control for global operations

Chapter 8: Marketing and Promotion in International Markets
8.1 Crafting a global marketing strategy
8.2 Leveraging digital marketing for international reach
8.3 Cultural considerations in advertising and promotion

Chapter 9: Risk Management and Adaptability
9.1 Identifying and mitigating risks associated with international trade
9.2 Strategies for adapting to changing market conditions
9.3 Highlighting companies that successfully navigated challenges

Chapter 1

Introduction

In a time described by globalization and interconnected economies, organizations are progressively perceiving the significance of extending their points of view past homegrown limits. The quest for learning experiences and the mission for upper hands have driven undertakings to investigate worldwide business sectors. In this mind boggling scene of worldwide business, conceiving powerful commodity techniques becomes fundamental for organizations planning to effectively explore the intricacies of global exchange.

The expression "send out procedures" embodies a multi-layered approach that organizations utilize to wander into and flourish in global business sectors. It incorporates a range of choices and activities that length statistical surveying, item variation, evaluating systems, calculated contemplations, and consistence with different administrative structures. As associations rise above topographical boundaries, they experience a plenty of difficulties and open doors, each requesting a nuanced and informed reaction.

At its center, a commodity procedure includes a smart and precise arrangement to acquaint items or administrations with unfamiliar business sectors. This endeavor requires a far reaching comprehension of the objective business sectors, including social subtleties, financial circumstances, lawful prerequisites, and cutthroat scenes. The complexities of worldwide exchange require an essential standpoint that goes past conventional plans of action, encouraging organizations to adjust and improve to stay significant and serious.

The worldwide commercial center is portrayed by its dynamism and unpredictability, and effective route through these intricacies requires a very much created send out procedure. As organizations set out on this excursion, they should wrestle with questions relating to showcase determination, risk relief, and the arrangement of their contributions with the different necessities and inclinations of global purchasers. Making a strong commodity system requests a mix of prescience, versatility, and a sharp comprehension of the interaction among worldwide and neighborhood elements.

This investigation into trade methodologies isn't just a scholarly activity; rather, it is a logical reaction to the developing idea of global business. Ventures are constrained to grow their domain past public lines to take advantage of new client bases, enhance income streams, and influence economies of scale. Be that as it may, this extension isn't without challenges. The intricacies of worldwide exchange, social varieties, administrative incongruities, and the requirement for customized promoting approaches require a deliberate and very much educated way to deal with trade techniques.

One of the crucial contemplations in trade technique advancement is the ID and assessment of target markets. The choice of business sectors assumes a urgent part in deciding the achievement or disappointment of a worldwide endeavor. Organizations should gauge factors, for example, market size, development potential, rivalry, social similarity, and administrative conditions. The course of market determination requires a nuanced comprehension of worldwide monetary patterns and a capacity to perceive arising open doors in different corners of the world.

Besides, the globalization of supply chains and the simplicity of correspondence have prompted expanded rivalry on a worldwide scale. Subsequently, organizations should fight with neighborhood contenders as well as face difficulties from worldwide players entering similar business sectors. In this hypercompetitive climate, a very much planned trade procedure turns into a vital device for cutting out a specialty and supporting an upper hand.

Adjusting items or administrations to fulfill the extraordinary needs of global business sectors is one more basic feature of commodity system. This includes a cautious assessment of social inclinations, administrative necessities, and specialized norms in the objective market. Fruitful global organizations are those that can fit their contributions to suit the particular necessities and assumptions for assorted buyer bases while keeping up with the guiding principle suggestion of their items or administrations.

Valuing procedures with regards to worldwide exchange are similarly many-sided. Factors like money changes, nearby evaluating standards, and the apparent worth of items or administrations in various business sectors should be thought of. Finding some kind of harmony among seriousness and benefit is a sensitive errand that requires an intensive comprehension of both worldwide financial patterns and nearby economic situations.

Calculated contemplations represent extra difficulties for organizations wandering into global business sectors. Proficient production network the executives, transportation coordinated operations, and dispersion networks are fundamental parts of an effective commodity technique. The capacity to convey items dependably and ideal to clients across borders is a deciding variable in building trust and supporting consumer loyalty.

Moreover, consistence with different administrative systems is a non-debatable part of global business. Every nation has its own arrangement of rules and guidelines administering imports, customs systems, and item norms. Exploring this intricate snare of guidelines requests a careful methodology, with organizations frequently depending on legitimate skill and vital associations to guarantee consistence while limiting interruptions to their tasks.

Risk the board is an intrinsic piece of any business attempt, yet it takes on added importance with regards to worldwide exchange. Political flimsiness, financial slumps, money vacillations, and unanticipated occasions, for example, cataclysmic events can present huge dangers to worldwide tasks.

Fostering an exhaustive gamble relief methodology is basic for organizations trying to defend their ventures and guarantee the congruity of their tasks in unfamiliar business sectors.

The job of innovation in send out methodologies couldn't possibly be more significant. In a period of computerized change, innovation fills in as an empowering agent, giving apparatuses and stages that work with correspondence, statistical surveying, production network the board, and online business. Embracing mechanical headways isn't simply a question of comfort; it is an essential basic for remaining cutthroat in the worldwide commercial center.

The elements of global exchange likewise require a nuanced way to deal with showcasing and brand the board. Social awareness, etymological contemplations, and a comprehension of neighborhood shopper conduct are critical for successful correspondence and brand situating. Organizations should be capable at creating advertising messages that resound with different crowds while keeping up with the validness and honesty of their image.

The advancing scene of worldwide exchange is set apart by local exchange alliances, peaceful accords, and international contemplations that shape the forms of global business. Grasping the international scene and keeping up to date with international improvements is fundamental for organizations trying to expect changes in market elements, administrative conditions, and exchange relations.

Cooperation and associations are progressively becoming key parts of effective product methodologies. Shaping collusions with neighborhood organizations, utilizing the skill of worldwide exchange affiliations, and building cooperative associations with wholesalers and retailers in target markets can improve an organization's market entrance and speed up its development in global business sectors.

As organizations wrestle with the complexities of commodity methodologies, the job of human resources can't be ignored. Building a group with the right range of abilities and social skills is crucial for executing global procedures successfully. Multifaceted relational abilities, worldwide market information, and a capacity to explore different business conditions are characteristics that add to the outcome of people and groups participated in global business.

All in all, the quest for worldwide business sectors requires a comprehensive and key way to deal with send out systems. The difficulties and open doors innate in worldwide exchange require a nuanced comprehension of market elements, social varieties, administrative scenes, and the developing idea of global business. Making and executing compelling commodity systems is definitely not a one-size-fits-all undertaking; all things being equal, it requests versatility, prescience, and a pledge to constant learning and development.

As organizations adventure into the mind boggling domain of global exchange, they should perceive that trade techniques are not static outlines but rather powerful guides that develop in light of evolving conditions. The capacity to explore the vulnerabilities of the worldwide commercial center, benefit from arising potential open doors, and relieve chances is a sign of fruitful global organizations. In this steadily developing scene, the plan and execution of product methodologies stand as a demonstration of an association's spryness, versatility, and key sharpness chasing practical development on the worldwide stage.

1.1 Brief overview of the importance of international markets for businesses

In the contemporary scene of business, the significance of worldwide business sectors couldn't possibly be more significant. As the world turns out to be progressively interconnected, organizations are constrained to extend their points of view past homegrown boundaries in quest for development, expansion, and reasonable achievement. The worldwide commercial center offers a plenty of chances for organizations to take advantage of new client bases, access extra income streams, and influence economies of scale. Understanding the meaning of global business sectors isn't only a hypothetical activity however an essential basic for organizations trying to flourish in a climate described by powerful financial powers and quick mechanical progressions.

At its center, wandering into worldwide business sectors empowers organizations to open new roads for development. Homegrown business sectors, while urgent, frequently have limits as far as market size and development potential. Conversely, worldwide business sectors offer an immense and various client base, introducing open doors for development that are not promptly accessible inside the bounds of a solitary country. Organizations that decisively position themselves in worldwide business sectors can accomplish economies of scale, drive higher deals volumes, and eventually improve their general productivity.

Expansion is one more convincing justification for organizations to investigate global business sectors. Reliance on a solitary market opens organizations to the dangers related with monetary vacillations, administrative changes, and neighborhood market elements. By enhancing their geological presence, organizations can moderate dangers and make a stronger and manageable activity. This broadening system turns out to be especially vital during times of financial vulnerability, as it gives a cradle against the difficulties that might be intended for specific locales or nations.

Worldwide business sectors likewise offer organizations the valuable chance to take advantage of new and developing business sectors. As economies advance and purchaser ways of behaving change, being at the very front of developing business sectors positions organizations for long haul achievement.

Early passage into these business sectors permits organizations to lay out brand presence, fabricate client devotion, and gain an upper hand over late participants. Moreover, organizations that explore the intricacies of developing business sectors effectively can partake in a first-mover benefit and shape the business scene in support of themselves.

Admittance to assets and unrefined components is a critical driver for organizations to wander into global business sectors. Certain districts might have bountiful assets or particular abilities that are crucial for explicit ventures. By laying out a presence in these districts, organizations can get a solid store network, lessen creation expenses, and gain an upper hand. This essential methodology is particularly important in enterprises where admittance to explicit data sources is basic for keeping up with quality and productivity.

Globalization has changed the manner in which organizations work, and worldwide business sectors act as a stage for joint effort and development. Through cross-line associations, organizations can get to integral assets, share information, and influence the mastery of neighborhood accomplices. Cooperative endeavors empower organizations to explore the complexities of unfamiliar business sectors all the more really, gain by nearby bits of knowledge, and adjust their methodologies to line up with social subtleties. Fundamentally, worldwide business sectors cultivate a culture of development and common advantage, driving advancement and seriousness in the worldwide business field.

The approach of innovation has additionally intensified the significance of worldwide business sectors for organizations. The simplicity of correspondence, headways in transportation, and the ascent of computerized stages have successfully diminished the boundaries to section into unfamiliar business sectors. Little and medium-sized undertakings (SMEs), specifically, presently have the valuable chance to partake in worldwide exchange and contend on a global scale. Innovation works with market section as well as empowers organizations to accumulate constant information, direct statistical surveying, and carry out deft procedures that answer changing business sector elements.

In addition, the interconnectivity of worldwide business sectors has suggestions for production network versatility. Ongoing occasions, like the Coronavirus pandemic, have highlighted the weaknesses of excessively focused supply chains. Organizations that source parts or depend on assembling processes in a solitary district face elevated takes a chance during disturbances. Broadening supply chains across various nations and locales upgrades flexibility, guaranteeing that organizations can adjust to unexpected difficulties and keep up with functional congruity.

The essential significance of worldwide business sectors is clear chasing vital unions and organizations. Coordinated efforts with worldwide elements, whether through joint endeavors, consolidations, or vital collusions, can enhance an organization's capacities and market reach. These associations frequently work with admittance to neighborhood mastery, dissemination organizations, and laid out client bases.

Key partnerships are a demonstration of the acknowledgment that prevailing in global business sectors requires monetary ventures as well as a profound comprehension of neighborhood elements and market subtleties.

Moreover, the meaning of worldwide business sectors reaches out past prompt monetary profits. It assumes a crucial part in cultivating social trade and understanding. Organizations that draw in with assorted markets gain openness to various social standards, buyer inclinations, and strategic approaches. This social knowledge is important, as it empowers organizations to tailor their items, administrations, and advertising systems to reverberate with neighborhood crowds. In doing as such, organizations upgrade their market pertinence as well as add to worldwide amicability and shared understanding.

According to a macroeconomic viewpoint, the commitment of organizations in global business sectors adds to the development and improvement of economies. Unfamiliar direct venture (FDI) and global exchange animate financial action, set out work open doors, and cultivate innovative exchange. The progression of merchandise, administrations, and capital across borders benefits individual organizations as well as adds to the general flourishing of countries. Legislatures frequently urge organizations to investigate global business sectors as a feature of their monetary improvement techniques, perceiving the positive overflow impacts on work, development, and foundation.

While the advantages of worldwide business sectors are significant, it is fundamental to recognize the inborn difficulties and intricacies related with worldwide business tasks. Diverse contrasts, administrative varieties, money gambles, and international vulnerabilities can present considerable snags. Fruitful commitment to global business sectors requires a nuanced comprehension of these moves and the improvement of methodologies to relieve related chances.

All in all, the significance of worldwide business sectors for organizations rises above simple extension; an essential basic characterizes the direction of progress in a globalized world. The quest for global business sectors is driven by the mission for development, broadening, admittance to assets, and cooperation. Organizations that explore the intricacies of worldwide business sectors effectively position themselves for supported achievement, flexibility, and importance in an always advancing financial scene. As the world keeps on seeing exceptional changes, the job of global business sectors stays fundamental to the essential vision of organizations meaning to blossom with the worldwide stage.

1.2 Key reasons for adopting export strategies

EXPORT STRATEGIES

The reception of commodity procedures is a critical choice for organizations looking to grow their span and exploit potential open doors past homegrown boundaries. This essential decision is spurred by a juncture of variables that by and large highlight the meaning of taking part in worldwide exchange.

From opening new income streams to moderating dangers and utilizing worldwide seriousness, the vital explanations behind taking on send out procedures are instrumental in forming the direction of organizations in the unique scene of worldwide business.

At the very front of purposes behind embracing send out methodologies is the quest for development and market extension. Homegrown business sectors, while fundamental, frequently present impediments as far as market size and immersion. By wandering into worldwide business sectors, organizations can take advantage of a tremendous and various pool of shoppers, subsequently fundamentally expanding their potential client base. This extension permits organizations to accomplish economies of scale, drive higher deals volumes, and at last add to the supported development and productivity of the business.

Expansion stands apart as one more convincing justification for organizations to take on trade methodologies. Overreliance on a solitary market opens organizations to different dangers, including financial slumps, administrative changes, and changes in customer inclinations. Expanding into worldwide business sectors gives a cushion against these dangers by spreading tasks across various districts. This essential methodology improves versatility and guarantees that the business isn't excessively reliant upon the fortunes of any single market, shielding against the antagonistic effects of limited difficulties.

Admittance to new and developing business sectors is a main impetus behind the choice to take on trade techniques. As economies develop and purchaser ways of behaving change, organizations that position themselves in developing business sectors gain a first-mover advantage. Early passage permits organizations to lay out brand presence, construct client dependability, and shape market patterns. The capacity to recognize and profit by arising open doors is a key upper hand that trade systems empower, permitting organizations to remain on the ball in a quickly developing worldwide business scene.

Vital asset procurement is a significant part of product methodologies. Certain locales might have plentiful assets, particular abilities, or mechanical aptitude that are pivotal for explicit businesses. By venturing into these districts, organizations can get a solid store network, lessen creation expenses, and gain an upper hand. This asset driven approach is especially pertinent in businesses where admittance to explicit data sources is basic for keeping up with quality and proficiency.

Additionally, the reception of commodity methodologies is driven by the basic to use worldwide seriousness. In a time of expanded globalization, organizations are contending with neighborhood rivals as well as confronting difficulties from worldwide players entering similar business sectors. Taking part in worldwide exchange forces organizations to upgrade their seriousness by advancing their items, administrations, and activities. The openness to different business sectors encourages development and proficiency, situating organizations to contend successfully on a worldwide scale.

Innovation assumes an essential part in the choice to take on trade systems. The simplicity of correspondence, headways in transportation, and the ascent of computerized stages have fundamentally decreased the boundaries to passage into unfamiliar business sectors. Innovation works with market section, empowering organizations to associate with worldwide clients, lead statistical surveying, and carry out coordinated systems. The computerized change has democratized admittance to worldwide business sectors, engaging even little and medium-sized undertakings (SMEs) to take part in worldwide exchange and contend universally.

Risk relief is a central thought that spurs organizations to embrace trade techniques. While global business sectors present worthwhile open doors, they likewise accompany intrinsic dangers, including political shakiness, monetary variances, and cash unpredictability. Expanding across various business sectors permits organizations to spread these dangers, limiting the effect of restricted difficulties. Strong product procedures incorporate gamble evaluation and alleviation measures, guaranteeing that organizations can explore vulnerabilities and defend their tasks in the worldwide field.

The quest for cost streamlining is an even minded justification behind organizations to embrace trade techniques. Working on a worldwide scale can give cost benefits through variables, for example, economies of scale, admittance to financially savvy inputs, and streamlined store network the executives. By smoothing out tasks and utilizing efficiencies acquired from worldwide exchange, organizations can upgrade their expense seriousness and work on in general productivity.

The coming of international alliances and worldwide joint efforts has further boosted the reception of commodity systems. Legislatures all over the planet have perceived the financial advantages of global exchange and have effectively participated in respective and multilateral arrangements to work with cross-line business. Organizations that decisively adjust their commodity methodologies to these arrangements can acquire special treatment, diminished exchange boundaries, and improved market access, establishing a good climate for development and extension.

Advancement and information move are necessary parts of taking on send out methodologies. Drawing in with global business sectors opens organizations to different viewpoints, mechanical progressions, and imaginative practices. Joint efforts with global accomplices work with the trading of information, thoughts, and best works on, driving development inside the association. The culturally diverse learning inborn in trade procedures adds to the improvement of a dynamic and versatile hierarchical culture, encouraging imagination and flexibility.

Brand building and worldwide perceivability are convincing drivers for organizations to take on trade systems. Laying out a presence in worldwide business sectors grows the client base as well as upgrades the brand's perceivability on a worldwide scale. The internationalization of a brand can add to its renown, validity, and saw esteem.

Organizations that effectively explore worldwide business sectors frequently appreciate improved memorability, making a positive input circle that further reinforces their market position.

The basic for feasible strategic approaches is progressively impacting the reception of product methodologies. Global business sectors are turning out to be seriously knowing, and purchasers are putting more prominent accentuation on earth and socially mindful strategic policies. Organizations that embrace send out methodologies with a guarantee to maintainability could not just meet developing buyer assumptions at any point yet additionally gain an upper hand. Manageability contemplations are woven into send out methodologies, enveloping moral obtaining, naturally cognizant creation, and dependable business direct.

Political and monetary solidness is a key element that organizations consider while taking on trade methodologies. While worldwide business sectors present open doors, they likewise present difficulties connected with international vulnerabilities, exchange pressures, and administrative changes. Organizations cautiously survey the political and monetary scenes of target markets to measure soundness and evaluate possible dangers. A stable political and monetary climate is helpful for effective worldwide tasks, giving an establishment to reasonable development and long haul achievement.

The job of commodity procedures in encouraging social trade and understanding can't be disregarded. Organizations that draw in with assorted markets gain openness to various social standards, customer ways of behaving, and strategic approaches. This social knowledge isn't just important for fitting items and administrations to reverberate with neighborhood crowds yet additionally adds to building generosity and cultivating positive connections. Social awareness turns into a basic piece of commodity techniques, guaranteeing that organizations explore worldwide business sectors with deference and flexibility.

The effect of product procedures on work creation and financial advancement is critical. As organizations venture into global business sectors, they frequently lay out neighborhood tasks, set out work open doors, and add to the financial advancement of host nations. Unfamiliar direct venture (FDI) driven by send out techniques animates monetary movement, foundation improvement, and the exchange of abilities and information. Legislatures, perceiving the positive overflow impacts, frequently urge organizations to embrace send out procedures as a component of their monetary improvement strategies.

All in all, the reception of product techniques is a complex choice driven by a mix of key goals and functional contemplations. From opening learning experiences and differentiating market presence to moderating dangers and utilizing worldwide seriousness, organizations set out on global exchange ventures with a reasonable comprehension of the advantages in question.

In this present reality where lines are progressively permeable, the reception of commodity methodologies isn't simply a strategic move yet an essential need for organizations seeking to flourish in the dynamic and interconnected worldwide commercial center.

1.3 Challenges and opportunities in global trade

The scene of worldwide exchange is set apart by a mind boggling interchange of difficulties and potential open doors that shape the methodologies and tasks of organizations on a worldwide scale. As organizations try to grow their compass and exploit the advantages of worldwide business, they should explore a powerful climate portrayed by financial, international, and mechanical powers. Understanding the subtleties of the difficulties and amazing open doors innate in worldwide exchange is fundamental for organizations to figure out informed procedures, adjust to evolving conditions, and prevail in the complexities of the worldwide commercial center.

Challenges in Worldwide Exchange:

Exchange Hindrances and Levies:

One of the essential difficulties in worldwide exchange is the presence of exchange hindrances and levies. Countries force different limitations, levies, and non-levy boundaries on imports to safeguard homegrown enterprises and manage exchange. Exploring these obstructions can fundamentally influence the expense construction and market access for organizations, expecting them to plan really to stay cutthroat.

Administrative Intricacy:

Worldwide exchange includes consistence with a horde of guidelines, going from customs techniques and documentation necessities to item norms and wellbeing guidelines. The assorted administrative structures across various nations request fastidious tender loving care and frequently require legitimate aptitude to guarantee consistence. Resistance can prompt deferrals, fines, and reputational harm.

Cash Variances:

Cash unpredictability represents an impressive gamble in worldwide exchange. Conversion scale changes can affect the expense of merchandise, adjust net revenues, and impact the seriousness of items in unfamiliar business sectors. Organizations participated in global exchange should carry out risk relief procedures, like supporting, to deal with the vulnerabilities related with cash variances.

Political Unsteadiness:

Political unsteadiness in various locales represents a huge test for organizations took part in worldwide exchange. Political vulnerabilities, changes in government strategies, and international strains can disturb supply chains, make market vulnerabilities, and unfavorably influence business tasks. Organizations need to screen international turns of events and foster emergency courses of action to relieve the effect of political insecurity.

Strategic Intricacies:
Productive operations are critical for effective worldwide exchange. Nonetheless, calculated intricacies, for example, transportation challenges, customs freedom deferrals, and production network interruptions can block the smooth progression of merchandise. Organizations should put resources into vigorous inventory network the executives and coordinated factors foundation to explore these difficulties and guarantee ideal conveyances.

Social and Language Obstructions:
Social subtleties and language contrasts present difficulties in correspondence, advertising, and relationship-working in worldwide business sectors. Misconceptions or social obtuseness can obstruct business exchanges and effect the progress of market passage techniques. Organizations need to put resources into multifaceted preparation and utilize nearby aptitude to actually explore these hindrances.

Licensed innovation Insurance:
Safeguarding protected innovation (IP) freedoms is a basic test in worldwide exchange. Various nations have shifting degrees of IP assurance, and exploring the intricacies of worldwide IP regulations is fundamental for organizations to defend their advancements, brands, and restrictive innovations. IP encroachment gambles with increment while working in assorted markets with differing lawful norms.

Store network Dangers:
Worldwide stockpile affixes are powerless to different dangers, including cataclysmic events, political agitation, and worldwide wellbeing emergencies. Occasions, for example, the Coronavirus pandemic featured the weaknesses of interconnected supply chains. Organizations need to survey and relieve store network takes a chance by enhancing providers, carrying out alternate courses of action, and utilizing innovation for constant perceivability.

Consistence with Maintainability Guidelines:
Expanding accentuation on maintainability and natural guidelines presents a test for organizations took part in worldwide exchange. Meeting assorted manageability guidelines, complying to eco-accommodating practices, and tending to buyer interest for morally obtained items require key preparation and transformation of strategic approaches to line up with worldwide supportability objectives.

Monetary Slumps and Market Unpredictability:
Worldwide monetary slumps, downturns, and market unpredictability present difficulties for organizations working in global business sectors. Vacillations in purchaser interest, changes in buying power, and financial vulnerabilities influence organizations' income streams and productivity. Powerful gamble the executives techniques are fundamental to effectively explore financial slumps.

Valuable open doors in Worldwide Exchange:
Market Extension and Broadening:

One of the essential open doors in worldwide exchange is the potential for market development and broadening. Organizations can take advantage of new client bases, investigate developing business sectors, and diminish reliance on a solitary market. Differentiating market presence upgrades flexibility and gives a stage to supported development.

Economies of Scale:

Taking part in worldwide exchange permits organizations to accomplish economies of scale by creating labor and products in bigger amounts. Bigger creation volumes frequently lead to cost efficiencies, lower unit costs, and further developed intensity. Organizations can advance their tasks and improve cost-viability through worldwide development.

Admittance to Particular Assets:

Worldwide exchange empowers organizations to get to specific assets, abilities, and advancements accessible in various districts. Certain nations might have extraordinary abilities or bountiful assets that are significant for explicit enterprises. By venturing into these locales, organizations can upgrade their upper hand and improve their worth chain.

Innovative Headways:

The fast speed of mechanical headways presents valuable open doors for organizations participated in worldwide exchange. Digitalization, mechanization, and the utilization of trend setting innovations work with productive correspondence, smooth out store network processes, and empower organizations to acquire an upper hand. Embracing mechanical advancements improves functional effectiveness and responsiveness.

Vital Collusions and Coordinated efforts:

Worldwide exchange gives valuable open doors to organizations to frame vital collusions and coordinated efforts with worldwide accomplices. Organizations with nearby organizations, joint endeavors, and cooperative endeavors empower admittance to neighborhood mastery, appropriation organizations, and market bits of knowledge. Such partnerships can upgrade market entrance and speed up development in unfamiliar business sectors.

Development and Information Move:

Openness to assorted markets cultivates development and information move. Organizations took part in worldwide exchange can profit from the trading of thoughts, best practices, and mechanical headways. Teaming up with global accomplices works with culturally diverse learning and improves the imaginative capacities of organizations.

Brand Building and Worldwide Acknowledgment:

Laying out a presence in worldwide business sectors adds to mark building and worldwide acknowledgment.

Organizations that effectively explore worldwide exchange frequently appreciate upgraded brand perceivability and validity. The internationalization of a brand can prompt expanded buyer trust and unwaveringness, making a positive criticism circle that fortifies market position.

Enhancement of Supply Chains:
Worldwide exchange permits organizations to enhance their inventory chains across various districts. Broadening limits the dangers related with confined disturbances, guaranteeing congruity in the stock of labor and products. Vital expansion improves production network versatility and adds to by and large business supportability.

Admittance to Monetary Open doors:
Taking part in worldwide exchange gives admittance to different monetary open doors. Organizations can investigate unfamiliar venture, access worldwide capital business sectors, and advantage from funding choices intended for specific districts. Worldwide monetary business sectors offer roads for organizations to streamline their capital construction and backing vital drives.

Commitment to Financial Turn of events:
Organizations engaged with worldwide exchange add to financial improvement at both nearby and worldwide levels. Through unfamiliar direct speculation (FDI), work creation, and foundation advancement, organizations animate financial development in have nations. The positive overflow impacts of worldwide exchange reach out to upgraded expectations for everyday comforts and further developed framework.

Adjusting Difficulties and Amazing open doors:
Making progress in worldwide exchange requires a nuanced comprehension of how to offset the innate difficulties with the accessible open doors. Organizations should embrace an essential methodology that includes risk the executives, market knowledge, and versatility. Here are key contemplations for organizations trying to explore the intricacies of worldwide exchange:

Key Gamble The executives:
Organizations ought to carry out hearty gamble the executives systems to distinguish, evaluate, and relieve the different dangers related with worldwide exchange. This incorporates cash risk the board, store network versatility arranging, and alternate courses of action to address international vulnerabilities.

Market Insight and Exploration:
Top to bottom market knowledge and exploration are basic for organizations participated in worldwide exchange. An exhaustive comprehension of target markets, including administrative conditions, social subtleties, and shopper ways of behaving, illuminates successful market section methodologies and supports informed independent direction.

Versatility and Adaptability:
The capacity to adjust to changing conditions is a vital determinant of progress in worldwide exchange. Organizations should be nimble and adaptable, prepared

to change techniques in light of advancing business sector elements, international movements, and monetary changes. Deftness empowers organizations to immediately jump all over arising chances and explore difficulties actually.

Interest in Innovation:

Embracing mechanical progressions is basic for organizations working in worldwide business sectors. The reception of advanced apparatuses, information investigation, and computerization smoothes out tasks, upgrades proficiency, and works on generally speaking seriousness. Innovation likewise works with ongoing correspondence and joint effort with global accomplices.

Diverse Skill:

Creating multifaceted ability is fundamental for organizations to effectively explore assorted markets. Social awareness, viable correspondence techniques, and a comprehension of nearby traditions add to building positive associations with partners in global business sectors.

Maintainability Combination:

Incorporating maintainability contemplations into strategic policies isn't just a reaction to administrative prerequisites yet in addition an essential objective. Organizations that focus on manageability practices can separate themselves in the worldwide commercial center, living up to the assumptions of ecologically cognizant customers and administrative principles.

Key Collusions and Organizations:

Framing key coalitions and organizations with neighborhood organizations and worldwide substances upgrades market entrance and fortifies worldwide seriousness. Cooperative endeavors empower organizations to use corresponding assets, share dangers, and access the aptitude expected to effectively explore different business sectors.

Nonstop Development:

Organizations ought to encourage a culture of constant development to remain ahead in the serious worldwide scene. Development empowers organizations to adjust to changing buyer inclinations, innovative progressions, and market patterns. The quest for advancement positions organizations as industry pioneers and upgrades their strength despite worldwide difficulties.

All in all, worldwide exchange presents a unique scene portrayed by a horde of difficulties and potential open doors. Organizations that decisively explore this mind boggling climate stand to acquire from market development, broadening, and admittance to specific assets. Adjusting the difficulties of administrative intricacies, international vulnerabilities, and strategic complexities with the open doors for advancement, market acknowledgment, and monetary improvement requires an all encompassing and versatile methodology.

Effective commitment to worldwide exchange requests a pledge to vital preparation, constant learning, and a steady spotlight on making esteem in an interconnected and dynamic worldwide commercial center.

Worldwide exchange has turned into a necessary piece of the cutting edge financial scene, introducing a bunch of chances for organizations, nations, and people the same. The interconnectedness of economies has made a tremendous snare of potential outcomes, encouraging monetary development, development, and coordinated effort. In this period of globalization, where boundaries are no longer obstructions, potential open doors in worldwide exchange proliferate.

One of the essential open doors lies in the extension of market reach. Organizations currently get the opportunity to take advantage of business sectors past their homegrown boundaries, arriving at a different and immense purchaser base. This worldwide reach empowers organizations to differentiate their client socioeconomics, decrease reliance on a solitary market, and gain by the changing requests and inclinations of buyers around the world.

Additionally, worldwide exchange offers the possibility of cost enhancement. Through worldwide obtaining of materials and creation, organizations can exploit cost differentials in different areas. This takes into account more serious evaluating as well as works with admittance to excellent data sources that may not be promptly accessible locally. Thus, organizations can upgrade their productivity, diminish creation costs, and eventually work on their seriousness in the worldwide market.

Notwithstanding cost streamlining, worldwide exchange encourages advancement through the trading of thoughts, innovations, and ability. Joint effort on a global scale empowers the cross-fertilization of information and the reception of best practices from various areas of the planet. This sharing of thoughts speeds up mechanical headways, driving businesses forward and advancing a culture of ceaseless improvement.

The simple entry to a worldwide ability pool is one more convincing open door introduced by worldwide exchange. Organizations can use the abilities and skill of experts from different foundations, making a more powerful and imaginative labor force. This upgrades hierarchical capacities as well as adds to the improvement of a multicultural and comprehensive workplace.

Besides, worldwide exchange gives a stage to little and medium-sized ventures (SMEs) to flourish. With diminished passage boundaries and further developed availability, much more modest organizations can take part in worldwide exchange, extending their points of view past neighborhood markets. This democratization of exchange engages SMEs to contend on a worldwide scale, encouraging monetary development and occupation creation.

The ascent of web based business has altogether enhanced the amazing open doors in worldwide exchange. Online stages work with consistent cross-line exchanges, empowering organizations, everything being equal, to get to global business sectors no sweat. Internet business has changed the retail scene as well as opened up new roads for specialist organizations, creatives, and computerized business visionaries to contact a worldwide crowd.

In the domain of agribusiness, worldwide exchange offers agrarian makers the opportunity to enhance their business sectors and diminish reliance on nearby circumstances. Admittance to worldwide business sectors gives a cradle against the dangers related with environment changeability, bugs, and different elements that can influence neighborhood farming efficiency. Furthermore, it permits ranchers to profit by occasional varieties, guaranteeing a more steady pay.

The improvement of worldwide stock chains is a vital driver of chances in worldwide exchange. Supply chains have become progressively complex, including numerous nations in the creation cycle. This intricacy permits organizations to profit from near benefits in different phases of creation, prompting by and large productivity gains. In any case, the Coronavirus pandemic featured the weakness of such interconnected supply chains, provoking a reconsideration of their flexibility and versatility.

Also, worldwide exchange can possibly lift millions out of destitution by setting out business open doors and encouraging financial improvement in developing business sectors. As organizations grow their activities universally, they frequently put resources into framework, innovation, and preparing in the districts where they work. This, thusly, adds to the improvement of neighborhood economies, enabling networks and working on expectations for everyday comforts.

The progression of exchange strategies and the arrangement of provincial economic alliance further enhance the open doors in worldwide exchange. Diminished taxes and exchange boundaries work with smoother cross-line exchanges, empowering expanded exchange volumes. Territorial economic deals, like the European Association and the Relationship of Southeast Asian Countries (ASEAN), make coordinated markets that take into account more consistent development of merchandise, administrations, and capital.

The development of monetary frameworks and instruments plays had an essential impact in improving open doors in worldwide exchange. High level monetary advances, for example, blockchain and computerized monetary standards, add to the productivity, security, and straightforwardness of worldwide exchanges. These advancements moderate dangers related with cross-line installments, making worldwide exchange more open and dependable for organizations, everything being equal.

Notwithstanding the heap valuable open doors, worldwide exchange likewise presents difficulties that should be explored capably. One such test is the unpredictability in money trade rates. Changes in cash values can influence the expense of imports and products, influencing the productivity of organizations participated in worldwide exchange. To alleviate this gamble, organizations frequently utilize supporting procedures and intently screen cash markets.

Exchange pressures and international vulnerabilities are extra difficulties that organizations face in the worldwide exchange scene. Political questions and exchange obstructions can upset the progression of labor and products, making vulnerabilities for organizations and financial backers. Exploring these international difficulties requires a nuanced comprehension of worldwide relations and the capacity to adjust to evolving conditions.

The ecological effect of worldwide exchange is a developing worry that can't be disregarded. The expanded development of merchandise across borders adds to fossil fuel byproducts and natural corruption. As consciousness of environmental change strengthens, organizations are under expanding strain to take on manageable practices and decrease their carbon impression. This shift towards maintainability presents the two difficulties and open doors for organizations took part in worldwide exchange.

Licensed innovation assurance is one more perplexing issue in worldwide exchange. As organizations extend globally, safeguarding their licensed innovation becomes principal. Unique lawful structures and implementation components across nations can present difficulties to protecting licensed innovation privileges. Exploring this scene requires a hearty lawful system and proactive measures to forestall encroachment.

The continuous computerized change has presented network protection as a basic thought in worldwide exchange. The expanded dependence on computerized stages and information trade conveys organizations defenseless to digital intimidations and assaults. Guaranteeing the security of touchy data and keeping up with the honesty of computerized exchanges are basic for organizations participated in worldwide exchange.

The Coronavirus pandemic significantly affects worldwide exchange, featuring the two weaknesses and amazing open doors. Disturbances to supply chains, travel limitations, and changes in customer conduct have reshaped the worldwide exchange scene. Organizations that can adjust to these progressions and influence arising potential open doors, for example, the expanded interest for web based business and computerized administrations, stand to flourish in the post-pandemic world.

All in all, open doors in worldwide exchange are huge and different, offering the potential for financial development, development, and coordinated effort on a worldwide scale. Organizations that can explore the difficulties, embrace manageability, and influence arising advances will situate themselves to profit by the horde prospects introduced by the interconnected universe of worldwide exchange. As the scene keeps on developing, flexibility and key foreknowledge will be critical to opening the maximum capacity of the open doors in worldwide exchange.

Chapter 2

Understanding International Markets

Understanding global business sectors is a multi-layered try that requires a nuanced handle of monetary, social, political, and innovative elements. As the world turns out to be progressively interconnected, organizations, state run administrations, and people look to explore the intricacies of worldwide business sectors to profit by open doors and oversee chances. From the complexities of cross-line exchange to the impact of social subtleties on customer conduct, an extensive comprehension of worldwide business sectors is vital for progress in the worldwide field.

At the center of understanding worldwide business sectors is the acknowledgment of the assorted monetary scenes that exist across the globe. Monetary frameworks shift fundamentally from one country to another, going from unrestricted economy free enterprise to halfway arranged economies. The level of government mediation, the job of private endeavor, and the degree of monetary advancement are basic factors that shape the business climate in every country. Organizations should adjust their procedures to line up with the financial designs of the business sectors they work in, perceiving that a one-size-fits-all approach is seldom viable.

Money trade rates are fundamental to worldwide exchange and venture. Understanding what trade rates vary and the variables meaning for these changes is fundamental for organizations took part in cross-line exchanges. Conversion standard developments influence the expense of imports and commodities, influencing the intensity of items and the benefit of organizations. Monetary pointers, international occasions, and market feeling all assume a part in impacting trade rates, making it basic for organizations to remain informed and utilize risk the board procedures to relieve cash related chances.

Social mindfulness is a foundation of grasping global business sectors. Social subtleties, values, and ways of behaving shape buyer inclinations and buying choices. An item or promoting methodology that resounds well in one culture might not have a similar effect in another. Language, correspondence styles, and social images all add to the unpredictable embroidery of buyer conduct. Effective organizations put resources into social insight, leading careful statistical surveying to fit their items and informing to the particular social settings of their objective business sectors.

Political variables apply a critical effect on global business sectors. Political security, government strategies, and administrative systems influence the simplicity of carrying on with work in a specific country. Changes in political authority, economic accords, and strategic relations can present vulnerabilities that influence market elements. Organizations should cautiously evaluate the political environment in the business sectors they work in, expecting and adjusting to potential changes that might affect their tasks and benefit.

Legitimate contemplations are vital in global business sectors, where organizations should explore different general sets of laws and administrative systems. Legally binding arrangements, licensed innovation insurance, and consistence with nearby regulations are basic parts of worldwide business. The absence of an unmistakable comprehension of legitimate necessities can prompt expensive debates and risk the standing of organizations working in unfamiliar business sectors. Looking for legitimate advice and keeping up to date with advancing guidelines are fundamental parts of effectively exploring the lawful scene of worldwide business sectors.

Exchange obstructions and duties are urgent components that organizations should consider while working in global business sectors. Protectionist measures, for example, import taxes and amounts, can essentially affect the expense of products and breaking point market access. Economic deals and discussions between nations impact the predominance of these hindrances, establishing a powerful climate that organizations should screen intently. The new pattern towards territorial economic alliance, like the Exhaustive and Moderate Understanding for Transoceanic Association (CPTPP) and the Provincial Complete Financial Organization (RCEP), highlights the significance of remaining sensitive to advancing exchange elements.

Worldwide stockpile affixes are essential to understanding global business sectors, particularly in a time where creation processes are in many cases appropriated across various nations. Organizations should cautiously deal with their inventory chains, taking into account factors, for example, transportation costs, lead times, and international dangers. The Coronavirus pandemic featured the weaknesses of worldwide inventory chains, inciting organizations to rethink their strength and enhance obtaining methodologies. A powerful comprehension of store network elements is fundamental for relieving disturbances and guaranteeing the productive progression of labor and products.

Mechanical progressions assume a groundbreaking part in forming global business sectors. The ascent of web based business, advanced correspondence, and robotization has sped up the speed of globalization. Organizations that influence innovation gain an upper hand by upgrading effectiveness, contacting more extensive crowds, and adjusting to quickly developing business sector patterns. The openness of data and the speed of correspondence have evened the odds for organizations, everything being equal, giving exceptional open doors to advancement and market development.

Statistical surveying is a central component of figuring out global business sectors. Exhaustive market investigation empowers organizations to recognize valuable open doors, survey contest, and designer their systems to the particular necessities of target markets. Statistical surveying includes a scope of exercises, from dissecting segment patterns and shopper conduct to assessing the cutthroat scene and administrative climate. The profundity and precision of statistical surveying straightforwardly influence the viability of a business' worldwide extension system.

Section modes into worldwide business sectors fluctuate, and organizations should cautiously consider the most reasonable methodology in view of their assets, goals, and the attributes of the objective market. Sending out, permitting, diversifying, joint endeavors, and completely claimed auxiliaries are among the choices accessible. Every section mode accompanies its own arrangement of benefits and difficulties, requiring an insightful assessment of elements, for example, market size, social fit, and administrative necessities. Effective global development frequently includes an essential mix of passage modes custom fitted to the particular conditions of each market.

Understanding the serious scene is basic for progress in global business sectors. Organizations should evaluate direct contenders as well as possible substitutes and arising players. Serious knowledge includes gathering data on contenders' assets, shortcomings, procedures, and market situating. By understanding the serious powers at play, organizations can recognize open doors for separation, development, and vital coordinated effort to acquire an upper hand.

Emergency the board is an essential part of figuring out worldwide business sectors, especially notwithstanding startling occasions like cataclysmic events, international pressures, or wellbeing emergencies like the Coronavirus pandemic. Organizations should foster powerful emergency courses of action, including risk evaluations, production network expansion, and emergency correspondence procedures. The capacity to adjust quickly and really to unanticipated difficulties is a sign of fruitful worldwide organizations.

Relationship building is essential in worldwide business sectors, where trust and compatibility assume a pivotal part in business connections. Building solid associations with neighborhood accomplices, providers, and clients encourages a more profound comprehension of the market and upgrades the probability of long haul achievement. Organizing, social responsiveness, and powerful correspondence are fundamental parts of relationship working in worldwide business.

Corporate social obligation (CSR) is progressively significant with regards to global business sectors. Organizations are supposed to work morally, add to manageable turn of events, and address social and ecological worries. CSR drives line up with worldwide assumptions as well as add to building a positive brand picture. Organizations that incorporate CSR into their worldwide activities are better situated to explore the mind boggling scene of assorted markets.

The job of government and public approach in global business sectors couldn't possibly be more significant. Legislatures shape the business climate through arrangements connected with exchange, tax collection, work, and the climate. Organizations should draw in with legislatures at both the homegrown and global levels, supporting for arrangements that work with fair contest and maintainable strategic policies. Understanding the political and administrative scene is fundamental for exploring the intricacies of worldwide business sectors.

Monetary administration in worldwide business sectors requires a sharp comprehension of cash risk, capital streams, and monetary guidelines. Organizations should oversee money openness, improve capital construction, and agree with worldwide bookkeeping guidelines. The capacity to explore complex monetary scenes guarantees the productive portion of assets and upgrades monetary flexibility even with financial vulnerabilities.

Social strategy is an arising part of global business, perceiving the impact of social relations on monetary collaborations. Organizations that participate in social strategy assemble spans between countries, encouraging positive connections and setting out open doors for cooperation. Social responsiveness and a veritable appreciation for variety add to effective social discretion endeavors, upgrading a business' standing and situating in global business sectors.

2.1 Analysis of different international markets and their dynamics

Directing an intensive investigation of various worldwide business sectors and understanding their elements is a basic part of vital decision-production for organizations expecting to grow their worldwide impression. Each market presents extraordinary open doors, difficulties, and intricacies formed by financial, social, political, and innovative variables. To explore effectively in the worldwide scene, organizations should dig into an extensive examination of global business sectors, fitting their systems to the particular subtleties of every locale.

Monetary Investigation:

The monetary scene of a market is an essential thought, impacting both momentary strategic choices and long haul key preparation. Key financial markers, for example, Gross domestic product development, expansion rates, and joblessness rates give bits of knowledge into the general soundness of an economy. Moreover, the conveyance of abundance, pay levels, and customer spending designs are pivotal variables that influence the interest for labor and products. Understanding the monetary elements of a market assists organizations with surveying its true capacity for development and adjust their valuing and showcasing methodologies in like manner.

Market Size and Development Potential:

The size of a market and its development potential are crucial contemplations for organizations looking for extension. Bigger business sectors frequently offer scale benefits, however more modest, high-development markets might introduce specialty open doors.

Examining market size includes surveying the all out addressable market (Hat) and distinguishing the fragments that line up with the business' items or administrations. Besides, understanding the development direction of a market gives significant experiences into its future possibilities, assisting organizations with distributing assets decisively.

Purchaser Conduct and Inclinations:

Social factors essentially impact purchaser conduct and inclinations. Organizations should lead top to bottom social examinations to understand the qualities, convictions, and ways of life of the ideal interest group in every worldwide market. Fitting items, showcasing messages, and client encounters to line up with neighborhood social standards cultivates more prominent acknowledgment and reverberation. Multifaceted ability is fundamental in exploring the complexities of shopper conduct, permitting organizations to make contributions that reverberate with different crowds.

Administrative and Legitimate Climate:

The administrative and legitimate climate shifts across global business sectors, expecting organizations to explore different lawful structures. Consistence with nearby guidelines, permitting prerequisites, and adherence to protected innovation regulations are significant contemplations. Understanding the administrative scene assists organizations with alleviating legitimate dangers, guaranteeing that their activities line up with neighborhood regulations. Changes in guidelines or political scenes can influence market section techniques and continuous business tasks, requiring a proactive way to deal with legitimate consistence.

Political Strength and Hazard:

Political strength is a critical determinant of a market's engaging quality for global organizations. A stable world of politics cultivates certainty and diminishes vulnerabilities. In any case, political dangers like changes in authority, international strains, and strategy movements can present difficulties. Organizations should survey the political environment of each market, taking into account factors like law and order, government soundness, and strategic relations. Vigorous gamble the board procedures are fundamental for moderating political vulnerabilities and defending the progression of tasks.

Exchange Strategies and Duties:

The exchange strategies of a nation, including levies and economic deals, essentially influence global exchange. Organizations participated in cross-line exchanges should examine the overarching exchange arrangements to comprehend the expenses and boundaries related with bringing in or trading merchandise. Economic deals, like international alliances (FTAs) or customs associations, can offer benefits by lessening duties and working with smoother exchange. Then again, protectionist measures might inflate expenses and cutoff market access. Exploring exchange strategies is fundamental for advancing production network effectiveness and generally speaking seriousness.

Foundation and Planned operations:

The nature of foundation and planned operations capacities in a market straightforwardly influences the productivity of supply chains. Organizations should evaluate transportation organizations, correspondence foundation, and operations administrations to guarantee the smooth progression of merchandise and data. Advanced foundation can decrease lead times, lower transportation expenses, and improve generally speaking functional proficiency. Alternately, lacking framework might present difficulties and require key changes in store network the board.

Innovative Scene:

The mechanical scene of a market shapes buyer assumptions, impacts rivalry, and gives open doors to development. Organizations should investigate factors like web infiltration, portable innovation reception, and the administrative climate for arising advances. Utilizing innovation patterns empowers organizations to remain cutthroat, arrive at shoppers through computerized channels, and gain by headways in regions, for example, web based business, information examination, and mechanization.

Cutthroat Scene:

Understanding the cutthroat scene is fundamental for forming compelling business sector passage and situating systems. Examining contenders' assets, shortcomings, portion of the overall industry, and separation methodologies gives important bits of knowledge. Organizations should distinguish upper hands, survey likely dangers, and separate their contributions to hang out on the lookout. Also, understanding the elements of serious competition assists organizations with expecting market drifts and change their techniques likewise.

Social and Social Variables:

Social and social elements assume an essential part in forming customer inclinations and market elements. Organizations should dig into social subtleties, social patterns, and segment movements to tailor their items and promoting messages really. Factors like language, customs, normal practices, and ways of life impact buyer conduct. A profound comprehension of social and social elements empowers organizations to foster items and promoting efforts that resound with the interest group, cultivating more prominent acknowledgment and brand steadfastness.

Natural and Maintainability Contemplations:

The developing accentuation on natural supportability and corporate obligation has made it basic for organizations to think about the ecological effect of their activities. Various business sectors might have changing degrees of mindfulness and assumptions about reasonable practices. Organizations that proactively address natural worries add to worldwide manageability as well as upgrade their image picture and appeal to ecologically cognizant buyers.

Social and Political Patterns:

Social and political patterns can shape shopper perspectives and impact market elements. Organizations should screen advancing patterns connected with social issues, variety, and political belief systems. Adjusting to changing cultural assumptions and adjusting strategic policies to arising social and political patterns can upgrade a brand's pertinence and allure. Alternately, organizations that are harsh toward these patterns might confront reputational dangers and difficulties in associating with their interest group.

Wellbeing and Security Guidelines:

The Coronavirus pandemic highlighted the significance of wellbeing and security contemplations in global business sectors. Organizations should survey wellbeing and security guidelines, pandemic readiness, and general wellbeing framework in each market. The capacity to adjust to evolving wellbeing related difficulties, execute security conventions, and guarantee the prosperity of representatives and clients is significant for business congruity.

Cash Trade and Monetary Contemplations:

Vacillations in money trade rates can affect the expense of merchandise, net revenues, and generally monetary execution. Organizations took part in worldwide exchange should oversee cash takes a chance by utilizing supporting procedures and remaining informed about money market patterns. Furthermore, monetary contemplations incorporate factors like tax assessment, capital accessibility, and monetary market dependability. Sound monetary administration is fundamental for improving asset distribution and keeping up with monetary versatility in global business sectors.

Customer Security and Protection Guidelines:

Customer security and protection guidelines fluctuate across wards, expecting organizations to adjust their practices to agree with nearby regulations. Understanding shopper privileges, information assurance guidelines, and security assumptions is significant for building entrust with clients and keeping away from legitimate difficulties. As worries about information security develop all around the world, organizations should focus on consistence with guidelines connected with the assortment, stockpiling, and utilization of client information.

Emergency Readiness and Flexibility:

The capacity to explore emergencies, whether financial slumps, catastrophic events, or wellbeing crises, is a basic part of worldwide business. Organizations should foster powerful emergency readiness and versatility methodologies to moderate possible disturbances to activities. This includes situation arranging, inventory network broadening, and the execution of possibility measures. Proactive emergency the board upgrades a business' capacity to adjust quickly and keep up with coherence notwithstanding unexpected difficulties.

Neighborhood Associations and Relationship Building:

Building solid associations with neighborhood accomplices, partners, and networks is fundamental for outcome in worldwide business sectors. Neighborhood organizations give experiences into the market, work with smoother tasks, and add to a positive brand picture. Drawing in with nearby networks and understanding their necessitie encourages generosity and reinforces the business.

2.2 Cultural, economic, and political factors affecting market entry

Market passage is a basic stage for organizations hoping to venture into new domains, and it is molded by a large number of variables, each assuming a significant part in deciding the achievement or difficulties looked by an organization. Social, financial, and political variables are among the most compelling powers that effect market section procedures, requiring cautious examination and transformation to the particular states of the objective market.

Social Variables:

Social contemplations are basic in the domain of market passage, as they shape buyer conduct, inclinations, and assumptions. A profound comprehension of the nearby culture is fundamental for organizations to tailor their items, administrations, and promoting systems successfully. Language, customs, normal practices, and values all add to the social texture of a general public and essentially impact customer decisions.

Social awareness is especially urgent in ventures where the item or administration is intently attached to social practices or convictions. For instance, the food and refreshment industry should explore different culinary inclinations, dietary limitations, and dietary patterns. Effective market passage procedures include directing careful social examinations, drawing in with neighborhood specialists, and adjusting contributions to line up with the social setting.

Additionally, correspondence techniques should be sensitive to social subtleties. Language obstructions, correspondence styles, and the utilization of images or symbolism can influence how a brand is seen. Putting resources into multifaceted preparation for representatives and utilizing nearby mastery in advertising efforts can assist organizations explore these difficulties and assemble significant associations with the interest group.

Financial Variables:

Financial circumstances are foremost contemplations in market passage choices. A far reaching investigation of the objective market's monetary scene assists organizations with surveying open doors for development, estimating methodologies, and in general market plausibility. Key financial markers, for example, Gross domestic product per capita, expansion rates, and buyer spending, offer bits of knowledge into the buying power and monetary prosperity of the populace.

Market size and development potential are basic monetary variables that impact market passage systems. While bigger business sectors might offer scale benefits, more modest business sectors with high development rates might introduce specialty potential open doors. Surveying the financial strength of a market is fundamental, as monetary vulnerabilities can influence customer certainty and buying conduct.

Besides, pay dispersion and differences inside a market can have suggestions for item situating and estimating. Organizations should tailor their contributions to line up with the pay levels of the ideal interest group, taking into account whether to situate items as exceptional, mid-reach, or financial plan amicable. Adaptability in evaluating procedures permits organizations to adjust to different financial circumstances and take care of a more extensive buyer base.

Cash trade rates are key to financial contemplations in global market section. Vacillations in money values can influence the expense of imports and commodities, influencing the seriousness of items and the benefit of organizations. Creating compelling money risk the board techniques, like supporting, is essential for moderating monetary vulnerabilities related with unstable trade rates.

Political Elements:

The world of politics of an objective market significantly affects market passage techniques. Political dependability, government strategies, and administrative structures shape the simplicity of carrying on with work and impact the general business environment. Stable worlds of politics ingrain certainty among financial backers and organizations, cultivating a favorable climate for market section and long haul tasks.

Notwithstanding, political dangers are intrinsic in the global business scene. Changes in administration, changes in government arrangements, and international strains can present vulnerabilities and difficulties. Organizations should direct exhaustive political gamble appraisals, keeping up to date with political turns of events and understanding what they might mean for market elements.

Administrative contemplations are fundamental to political elements influencing market passage. Consistence with nearby regulations, permitting necessities, and adherence to industry-explicit guidelines are fundamental for guaranteeing lawful similarity. Exploring assorted lawful structures expects organizations to draw in with legitimate specialists, lay out straightforward cycles, and remain proactive in checking and adjusting to changes in guidelines.

Exchange arrangements and taxes are extra political elements that effect market section. International alliances (FTAs) and customs guidelines impact the simplicity of cross-line exchange.

Organizations should evaluate the overall exchange approaches to comprehend the expenses and boundaries related with bringing in or sending out merchandise. In addition, exchange pressures between nations can acquaint intricacies that organizations need with explore in a calculated manner.

Cooperation of Social, Financial, and Political Variables:

The exchange of social, financial, and political variables is unpredictable, and fruitful market passage methodologies require a comprehensive comprehension of their consolidated effect. For example, social inclinations might impact the sorts of items customers will buy, while monetary circumstances decide their reasonableness. At the

EXPORT STRATEGIES

same time, political dependability gives a positive climate to organizations to work and flourish.

Now and again, political variables may straightforwardly impact social angles. Government strategies or guidelines might direct social practices or limitations, affecting the agreeableness and market capability of specific items or administrations. Then again, social movements might provoke state run administrations to present new guidelines or adjust existing ones to line up with advancing cultural standards.

Monetary factors frequently go about as a scaffold among social and political contemplations. Monetary turn of events and pay levels add to social movements, impacting buyer desires and ways of life. Moreover, political strength and sound administration are vital for encouraging financial development, making a harmonious connection among monetary and political elements.

Globalization has additionally confounded the connection of these variables. As organizations grow universally, they experience different social scenes, financial circumstances, and worlds of politics. Adjusting to this variety requires a nuanced approach that perceives the interconnectedness of these elements and the requirement for adaptable, setting explicit market section procedures.

Vital Contemplations for Market Section:

Understanding the many-sided trap of social, monetary, and political variables requires an essential way to deal with market section. A few key contemplations can direct organizations in creating compelling business sector passage techniques:

Exhaustive Statistical surveying: Careful statistical surveying is primary to understanding social, monetary, and political elements. Inside and out investigations of shopper conduct, financial markers, and political scenes give the bits of knowledge expected to go with informed choices.

Social Knowledge: Creating social insight inside the association is fundamental. This includes understanding social subtleties as well as cultivating a social outlook that penetrates dynamic cycles. Multifaceted preparation for workers can upgrade social awareness and work with compelling commitment with different business sectors.

Versatile Showcasing Techniques: Advertising procedures should be versatile to nearby social inclinations and responsive qualities. Fitting publicizing messages, marking, and special missions to line up with social qualities improves the reverberation of a brand in the objective market.

Adaptability in Valuing: Financial contemplations require adaptability in estimating procedures. Organizations ought to be ready to change estimating models in light of the financial states of the objective market, taking into account factors, for example, pay levels, buying power, and neighborhood rivalry.

Lawful Consistence and Hazard The executives: Exploring different legitimate systems requests a proactive way to deal with legitimate consistence. Connecting with legitimate specialists, remaining informed about administrative changes, and carrying out powerful gamble the executives systems are pivotal for relieving lawful and political dangers.

Government Relations: Laying out certain associations with government specialists can add to a great business climate. Drawing in with nearby legislatures, industry affiliations, and significant partners upgrades a's comprehension business might interpret the political scene and positions it as a dependable corporate resident.

Vital Unions: Building key coalitions with nearby accomplices can work with smoother market passage. Neighborhood accomplices bring experiences into social subtleties, administrative scenes, and shopper conduct, offering important help for organizations exploring new domains.

Situation Arranging: Given the unique idea of worldwide business sectors, organizations ought to take part in situation wanting to expect possible changes in social, monetary, or political circumstances. This proactive methodology empowers organizations to adjust quickly to unexpected difficulties and open doors.

Contextual investigations:

Looking at genuine models delineates how social, monetary, and political elements impact market section techniques.

1. **McDonald's in India:**
   McDonald's fruitful passage into the Indian market features the significance of social variation. Perceiving the meaning of vegetarianism in Indian culture, McDonald's presented a menu with a significant extent of veggie lover choices. Also, the organization changed its menu to take care of nearby preferences, presenting things like the McAloo Tikki burger. By adjusting to social inclinations, McDonald's made acknowledgment and progress in a market known for its different culinary customs.
2. **Tesla in China:**
   Tesla's entrance into the Chinese market shows the effect of monetary variables on market passage. Perceiving the capability of the Chinese electric vehicle market, Tesla decisively situated itself to exploit government impetuses and sponsorships for electric vehicles. Utilizing monetary circumstances and positive strategies, Tesla laid out areas of strength for an in China, turning into a key part on the planet's biggest auto market.
3. **Airbnb's Worldwide Extension:**

Airbnb's worldwide extension exhibits the transaction of social, financial, and political variables. The stage's prosperity is attached in its capacity to adjust to assorted social assumptions about convenience and neighborliness. Monetary contemplations, like evaluating models and reasonableness, fluctuate across business sectors, affecting Airbnb's systems. Moreover, Airbnb has explored political difficulties, remembering administrative examination for different wards, by drawing in with nearby legislatures and adjusting its plan of action to conform to neighborhood guidelines.

2.3 Identification of potential target markets

The ID of potential objective business sectors is a vital stage for organizations intending to grow their scope and gain by new open doors. This interaction includes a thorough investigation of different variables to survey the reasonability and engaging quality of various business sectors. From segment contemplations to monetary pointers, organizations should explore an intricate scene to pinpoint the most reasonable business sectors for their items or administrations.

Segment Investigation:

Segment factors assume an essential part in distinguishing potential objective business sectors. Understanding the age, orientation, pay levels, schooling, and way of life of the populace assists organizations with fitting their items and advertising procedures. For example, an item taking care of the inclinations and requirements of a more youthful segment might make progress in business sectors with a huge youth populace. Segment examination gives experiences into the size and piece of the ideal interest group, empowering organizations to adjust their contributions to the qualities of the market.

Populace development rates and patterns are additionally significant contemplations. High populace development might show a developing business sector with expanding customer interest, while declining populace development might flag a soaked or mature market. Segment shifts, for example, urbanization or changes in family structures, can impact customer conduct and present new market potential open doors.

Financial Contemplations:

Financial variables are essential to the ID of potential objective business sectors. Examining the total national output (Gross domestic product), pay levels, and by and large financial strength of a locale gives experiences into the buying power and buyer spending limit. Markets with a developing working class and rising dispensable wages frequently present appealing open doors for organizations.

Pay circulation inside a populace is a basic monetary thought. Organizations should survey whether their items or administrations line up with the pay levels of the objective market. This includes assessing whether the market is more qualified for top notch, mid-reach, or financial plan well disposed contributions. Monetary contemplations additionally reach out to elements, for example, expansion rates, joblessness levels, and generally financial strength, which can influence shopper certainty and buying conduct.

Besides, surveying the financial strategies and business environment of a potential objective market is fundamental. Great monetary strategies that advance business venture, unfamiliar speculation, and market rivalry establish a favorable climate for business development. On the other hand, ominous monetary circumstances, administrative difficulties, or elevated degrees of debasement might present dangers and cutoff the engaging quality of a market.

Market Size and Development Potential:

The size and development capability of a market are basic variables in the ID of potential objective business sectors. A bigger market offers scale benefits and the potential for higher deals volumes. Notwithstanding, more modest business sectors with high development rates might give specialty valuable open doors to organizations to lay out serious areas of strength for an and catch a huge portion of the overall industry.

Dissecting the all out addressable market (Hat) includes assessing the possible interest for an item or administration in a given market. Organizations should survey factors, for example, populace size, purchaser inclinations, and rivalry to decide the versatility of their contributions. Moreover, assessing market patterns and estimates gives bits of knowledge into the future development direction of the objective market, assisting organizations with coming to informed conclusions about their market section techniques.

Cutthroat Scene:

An inside and out investigation of the cutthroat scene is fundamental for recognizing potential objective business sectors. Understanding existing contenders, their piece of the pie, qualities, shortcomings, and systems is critical for organizations to successfully situate themselves. A market with an elevated degree of contest might expect organizations to separate their contributions or take on extraordinary offering recommendations to stick out.

Contender examination likewise includes evaluating possible boundaries to passage, for example, solid brand reliability, high exchanging costs for shoppers, or select dissemination channels. Recognizing holes or neglected needs in the market permits organizations to fit their items or administrations to make up for those shortfalls, making an upper hand.

Also, organizations ought to consider the potential for problematic advances or new participants that could reshape the cutthroat scene. Expecting and adjusting to changes in the cutthroat climate is essential for long haul progress in an objective market.

Social and Social Elements:

Social and social variables assume a huge part in the ID of potential objective business sectors. Shopper conduct, inclinations, and buying choices are profoundly affected by social subtleties, values, and social patterns. Organizations should lead exhaustive social investigations to guarantee that their items or administrations line up with the social setting of the objective market.

Language contemplations are fundamental in global business sectors, where viable correspondence is fundamental for fruitful market passage. Adjusting promoting messages, marking, and item naming to the neighborhood language and social standards upgrades the acknowledgment and allure of a brand. Social responsiveness is basic for staying away from errors or inadvertent social blooper that could adversely influence the view of a business.

Social patterns, for example, way of life changes, ecological cognizance, or changes in buyer inclinations, ought to likewise be thought of. For instance, advertises that show a developing interest in maintainability might introduce valuable open doors for eco-accommodating items and drives. Recognizing and lining up with winning social patterns add to a business' significance and reverberation with the ideal interest group.

Mechanical Scene:

The mechanical scene of a potential objective market is a critical thought for organizations hoping to recognize valuable open doors. Headways in innovation can make new business sectors, upset existing enterprises, and impact buyer assumptions. Organizations should survey factors like web infiltration, cell phone utilization, and the reception of arising advancements inside the objective market.

Web based business patterns and the predominance of advanced installment strategies are especially important in the present interconnected world. A market with an elevated degree of digitalization might offer open doors for online deals and computerized showcasing. Organizations ought to assess the innovative framework and computerized preparation of a market to decide the plausibility of carrying out innovation driven systems.

In addition, understanding the mechanical inclinations and ways of behaving of the ideal interest group is vital. Shopper reception of new advancements, for example, brilliant gadgets or computerized stages, impacts how items and administrations are consumed and showcased. Organizations that line up with innovative patterns can acquire a strategic advantage and better interface with well informed customers.

Political and Administrative Climate:

The political and administrative climate essentially influences the ID of potential objective business sectors. Political strength is a basic component that encourages certainty among organizations and financial backers. Alternately, political precariousness, successive changes in administration, or international strains can present vulnerabilities and dangers that might influence market section procedures.

Administrative contemplations incorporate consistence with neighborhood regulations, industry-explicit guidelines, and principles. Organizations should evaluate the administrative scene to guarantee lawful congruity and stay away from possible legitimate difficulties. Understanding the simplicity of carrying on with work, tax collection strategies, and government motivators for unfamiliar venture gives bits of knowledge into the general business environment of a potential objective market.

Exchange approaches and duties are extra political elements that can impact market section choices. The presence of international alliances (FTAs) or customs associations might work with smoother cross-line exchange, while protectionist measures can inflate expenses and cutoff market access. Exploring the political and administrative scene requires a proactive way to deal with lawful consistence and an exhaustive comprehension of expected chances.

Geographic Contemplations:

The geographic qualities of a potential objective market are significant for organizations to survey calculated and circulation challenges. Factors like the size of the market, transportation framework, and geographic scattering of the main interest group influence the achievability of arriving at shoppers proficiently.

Openness and nearness to providers, creation offices, and dissemination channels impact inventory network the board. Organizations should assess the expense viability of strategies and transportation choices to decide the in general functional effectiveness in an objective market.

Also, geographic contemplations incorporate environment varieties that might influence item inclinations or occasional interest designs. Understanding the geographic setting permits organizations to tailor their methodologies to oblige provincial contrasts and improve asset distribution.

Buyer Conduct and Inclinations:

Examining shopper conduct and inclinations is integral to the ID of potential objective business sectors. Organizations should dig into the variables affecting buying choices, brand unwaveringness, and item assumptions. Statistical surveying, studies, and customer criticism give important experiences into the requirements and wants of the interest group.

Understanding the variables that drive buyer unwaveringness permits organizations to foster systems to fabricate and keep up serious areas of strength for with connections. Furthermore, distinguishing item elements or administrations that resound with customer inclinations empowers organizations to separate themselves on the lookout.

Social, monetary, and social variables add to customer conduct, and organizations should explore these elements to make contributions that line up with the qualities and assumptions for the objective market. By expecting and adjusting to purchaser inclinations, organizations can improve their market situating and appeal to the ideal interest group.

Risk Appraisal:

Leading an intensive gamble evaluation is a fundamental piece of distinguishing potential objective business sectors. Dangers can radiate from different sources, including financial vulnerabilities, political flimsiness, social false impressions, and administrative difficulties. Organizations should assess the potential dangers related with market passage and foster gamble alleviation procedures to shield their activities.

Risk appraisal implies situation intending to expect likely difficulties and disturbances. This proactive methodology empowers organizations to foster emergency courses of action, expand supply chains, and carry out measures to adjust quickly to unexpected conditions. Perceiving and tending to likely dangers in the beginning

EXPORT STRATEGIES

phases of market recognizable proof is essential for guaranteeing the manageability and strength of business tasks.

Market Section Systems:

When potential objective business sectors have been recognized, organizations should form powerful market passage systems. The decision of section mode, whether through sending out, permitting, diversifying, joint endeavors, or laying out entirely claimed auxiliaries, relies upon different variables, including the degree of hazard resilience, accessible assets, and the attributes of the objective market.

Trading is a typical passage mode for organizations hoping to enter worldwide business sectors. It includes offering items or administrations to an unfamiliar market without laying out an actual presence. Authorizing and diversifying permit organizations to use the brand and aptitude of nearby accomplices. Joint endeavors include cooperation with nearby substances, while completely possessed auxiliaries give full command over activities however require critical venture.

Market passage methodologies ought to line up with the distinguished objective business sectors and think about the exceptional qualities and difficulties of each market. Intensive preparation, statistical surveying, and an unmistakable comprehension of social, financial, and administrative elements add to the outcome of market passage techniques.

The distinguishing proof of potential objective business sectors is a multi-layered process that includes a complete investigation of segment, financial, social, innovative, political, and geographic elements. Organizations looking to extend their span should explore a perplexing scene to pinpoint showcases that offer open doors for development and line up with their items or administrations.

An all encompassing way to deal with market distinguishing proof includes figuring out the interconnectedness of these variables and perceiving their effect on buyer conduct, serious scenes, and by and large market plausibility. Social responsiveness, mechanical availability, and flexibility to financial and administrative circumstances are fundamental credits for organizations meaning to distinguish and enter potential objective business sectors effectively.

In addition, the course of market recognizable proof is dynamic, expecting organizations to remain sensitive to advancing patterns, customer inclinations, and worldwide turns of events. Ordinary reassessment of target markets permits organizations to adjust their techniques, exploit arising open doors, and explore difficulties successfully.

In a globalized and interconnected world, the capacity to recognize and enter potential objective business sectors decisively is a foundation of business achievement. By utilizing market insight, directing exhaustive examinations, and taking on adaptable and versatile procedures, organizations can situate themselves for feasible development and seriousness on the global stage.

Chapter 3

Market Research and Analysis

Statistical surveying and examination assume a urgent part in the achievement and maintainability of organizations across different businesses. As the business scene keeps on developing quickly, associations should remain receptive to showcase elements, shopper conduct, and industry patterns to settle on informed choices and keep an upper hand. This extensive interaction includes the methodical social event, understanding, and assessment of important information to reveal experiences that drive vital direction.

One of the essential targets of statistical surveying is to acquire a profound comprehension of the market wherein a business works. This includes concentrating on the interest group, contenders, and the more extensive industry. Thusly, organizations can recognize valuable open doors, evaluate possible dangers, and refine their methodologies to satisfy the consistently changing needs of the market.

Understanding the main interest group is a crucial part of statistical surveying. This includes digging into the socioeconomics, psychographics, and ways of behaving of the shoppers that a business intends to serve. Segment factors like age, orientation, pay, and area give fundamental experiences into the qualities of the objective market. Psychographic factors, then again, dig into the qualities, interests, and ways of life of the crowd, offering a more nuanced comprehension of their inclinations.

Shopper conduct is one more basic element of statistical surveying. Investigating how shoppers settle on buying choices, their purchasing behaviors, and variables impacting their decisions assists organizations with fitting their items or administrations to address client issues really. This understanding empowers the advancement of designated promoting methodologies that resound with the target group, eventually driving deals and cultivating brand unwaveringness.

Contender examination is similarly urgent in statistical surveying. Analyzing the qualities and shortcomings of contenders, understanding their market situating, and distinguishing possible holes in the market are crucial parts of this cycle. By benchmarking against industry rivals, organizations can refine their own procedures, separate themselves on the lookout, and benefit from potential chances to acquire an upper hand.

As well as understanding the market and ideal interest group, organizations should likewise screen industry patterns and changes. This includes keeping up to date with mechanical progressions, administrative turns of events, and changes in buyer inclinations.

By expecting and adjusting to these changes, associations can situate themselves as trend-setters and pioneers in their particular enterprises.

The techniques utilized in statistical surveying are different, going from customary ways to deal with state of the art advancements. Studies and polls are exemplary instruments for social occasion quantitative information, giving factual experiences into buyer inclinations and feelings. Center gatherings work with subjective exploration by cultivating inside and out conversations and uncovering nuanced viewpoints. In the computerized age, web examination and virtual entertainment checking offer constant information on buyer conduct and feeling.

Innovation has likewise brought about cutting edge information examination and man-made consciousness (simulated intelligence) applications in statistical surveying. Enormous information investigation empowers the handling of immense datasets to distinguish examples, patterns, and connections. AI calculations can anticipate purchaser conduct in light of authentic information, giving important bits of knowledge to vital navigation. The coordination of these innovations has changed statistical surveying, making it more effective, exact, and receptive to dynamic economic situations.

The significance of statistical surveying reaches out past the send off of new items or administrations. A nonstop cycle illuminates each stage regarding the business lifecycle. From distinguishing market valuable open doors and planning powerful promoting efforts to assessing the exhibition of existing items and expecting future patterns, statistical surveying is a directing power that shapes the direction of a business.

For new companies and independent ventures, statistical surveying is especially vital. Restricted assets make it basic to designate ventures carefully and center around systems that are probably going to yield positive outcomes. By leading exhaustive statistical surveying, these organizations can limit gambles, streamline asset distribution, and improve the probability of outcome in serious business sectors.

Laid out organizations likewise benefit essentially from continuous statistical surveying. As business sectors develop, customer inclinations shift, and new contenders arise, organizations should adjust to remain pertinent. Statistical surveying gives the bits of knowledge expected to change techniques, refine item contributions, and keep serious areas of strength for a position.

The globalization of business sectors further highlights the significance of statistical surveying. Organizations working on a worldwide scale should explore different social, financial, and administrative conditions. Understanding the novel attributes of each market is fundamental for fitting methodologies that reverberate with neighborhood purchasers and follow territorial guidelines.

Market division is a vital idea in statistical surveying, working with a more designated way to deal with serving different purchaser gatherings. By partitioning the market into sections in view of qualities like socioeconomics, conduct, or geology, organizations can tweak their advertising endeavors to more readily meet the particular necessities of each fragment. This upgrades the significance of items or administrations, increments consumer loyalty, and further develops in general business execution.

The approach of web based business and advanced showcasing has extended the roads through which organizations can lead statistical surveying. Online studies, web-based entertainment examination, and site examination give an abundance of information on buyer conduct in the computerized domain. Internet business stages themselves create significant information on buying designs, permitting organizations to upgrade their web-based presence and improve the client shopping experience.

In the domain of business-to-business (B2B) markets, statistical surveying is similarly crucial. Understanding the requirements and inclinations of corporate clients, distinguishing potential colleagues, and remaining informed about industry patterns are fundamental for progress in B2B conditions. Statistical surveying in B2B settings frequently includes a more particular and designated approach, taking into account the one of a kind elements of the business-to-business relationship.

The reconciliation of statistical surveying with key arranging is a sign of fruitful organizations. Key arranging includes putting forth long haul objectives, characterizing the moves toward accomplish them, and designating assets successfully. Statistical surveying gives the establishment to informed dynamic in essential preparation, guaranteeing that objectives are lined up with market real factors and that the picked procedures are appropriate to the cutthroat scene.

Development is a vital driver of progress in the present powerful business climate. Statistical surveying powers advancement by giving bits of knowledge into arising patterns, neglected buyer requirements, and regions where improvement is wanted. Organizations that focus on advancement influence statistical surveying to distinguish amazing open doors for item improvement, process improvement, and the making of interesting incentives.

The drug business embodies the basic job of statistical surveying in advancement. Innovative work (Research and development) in this area require significant ventures, and the outcome of new medications relies upon understanding business sector needs, administrative necessities, and the cutthroat scene. Statistical surveying guides drug organizations in distinguishing restorative regions with neglected needs, advancing clinical preliminary plans, and situating new medications actually on the lookout.

The effect of statistical surveying isn't restricted to the confidential area; it is likewise important for non-benefit associations and government organizations. In the non-benefit area, understanding contributor inclinations and cultural requirements is fundamental for powerful raising money and program improvement. Government organizations depend on statistical surveying to illuminate arrangements, designate assets, and address the advancing requirements of residents.

Moral contemplations are essential to the act of statistical surveying. The assortment and utilization of customer information raise security concerns, and organizations should stick to moral principles to fabricate and keep up with entrust with their crowds. Straightforwardness in information assortment works on, getting educated assent from members, and shielding information against unapproved access are fundamental components of moral statistical surveying.

The ascent of information security guidelines, like the Overall Information Assurance Guideline (GDPR) in Europe, highlights the significance of moral information rehearses. Organizations working worldwide should explore a complicated scene of guidelines to guarantee consistence with changing principles across various purviews. Moral statistical surveying lines up with legitimate necessities as well as adds to the foundation of a positive brand picture.

While the advantages of statistical surveying are significant, challenges exist in its execution. One normal test is the sheer volume of information accessible, frequently alluded to as data over-burden. Figuring out tremendous measures of information to extricate significant bits of knowledge requires progressed scientific instruments and mastery. Organizations should put resources into the right advancements and ability to explore this challenge really.

Another test is the requirement for constant experiences in the present high speed business climate. Customary statistical surveying techniques, for example, reviews and center gatherings, may not give the quickness expected to answer quickly changing economic situations. Organizations are progressively going to coordinated research approaches and progressed examination to get continuous bits of knowledge and remain in front of the opposition.

The worldwide idea of business sectors represents extra difficulties for organizations participated in global tasks. Social contrasts, language hindrances, and fluctuating purchaser ways of behaving require a nuanced way to deal with statistical surveying in various locales. Organizations should put resources into diverse ability and team up with nearby specialists to guarantee the precision and significance of their exploration discoveries.

Innovative headways, while upgrading the abilities of statistical surveying, additionally acquaint difficulties related with information security and trustworthiness. As organizations gather and store expanding measures of delicate purchaser information, the gamble of information breaks and digital assaults rises. Executing powerful network safety gauges and guaranteeing consistence with information insurance guidelines are basic to relieve these dangers.

The Coronavirus pandemic has additionally highlighted the requirement for organizations to adjust their statistical surveying methodologies. The pandemic has disturbed worldwide stockpile chains, modified buyer conduct, and sped up advanced change. Organizations that have been nimble in changing their statistical surveying approaches to represent these progressions have been exceptional situated to explore the difficulties presented by the pandemic.

Regardless of the difficulties, the fate of statistical surveying holds guarantee, driven by continuous mechanical headways and the rising acknowledgment of its essential worth. Man-made reasoning and AI will keep on assuming a focal part in mechanizing information examination, empowering organizations to proficiently determine noteworthy bits of knowledge more. The mix of expanded reality and computer generated reality into statistical surveying techniques might give vivid encounters to members, prompting more precise and true reactions.

As organizations embrace a more comprehensive way to deal with statistical surveying, the reconciliation of subjective and quantitative techniques will turn out to be progressively normal. Consolidating the profundity of experiences acquired from subjective exploration, for example, center gatherings and meetings, with the factual meticulousness of quantitative information investigation makes an extensive comprehension of the market scene.

The democratization of information and investigation is another pattern molding the eventual fate of statistical surveying. Easy to understand investigation stages and instruments enable non-specialists inside associations to get to and decipher information, democratizing the dynamic interaction. This shift decreases dependence on specific information investigators and cultivates a culture of information driven navigation across all levels of the association.

All in all, statistical surveying and examination are necessary parts of fruitful business system. From understanding the complexities of the interest group and observing industry patterns to directing development and illuminating vital preparation, statistical surveying gives the experiences expected to explore the intricacies of the advanced business scene. As innovation keeps on propelling, organizations should adjust their statistical surveying strategies to bridle the maximum capacity of information and investigation, guaranteeing they stay coordinated, cutthroat, and receptive to advancing business sector elements.

Moral contemplations and a guarantee to information protection are principal, as organizations endeavor to fabricate and keep up with entrust with their crowds in a time of expanding examination and administrative oversight. Notwithstanding the difficulties, the fate of statistical surveying holds energizing prospects, promising a more incorporated, effective, and democratized way to deal with understanding and molding the business sectors of tomorrow.

3.1 Importance of thorough market research before entering a new market

The significance of exhaustive statistical surveying prior to entering another market couldn't possibly be more significant. For organizations looking for extension or broadening, entering another market is an essential choice laden with difficulties and vulnerabilities. Without an exhaustive comprehension of the objective market, its elements, and the inclinations of its customers, a business gambles with committing exorbitant errors that can subvert its prosperity. Exhaustive statistical surveying fills in as the establishment for informed navigation, empowering organizations to evaluate valuable open doors, relieve dangers, and designer their procedures to the particular requests of the new market.

One of the essential justifications for why intensive statistical surveying is fundamental prior to entering another market is the variety of buyer inclinations and ways of behaving. Various business sectors have unmistakable social, social, and monetary settings that impact how customers connect with items and administrations. What might be a fruitful methodology in one market could crash and burn in another. Understanding the subtleties of purchaser conduct in the objective market is pivotal for fitting items, administrations, and showcasing procedures to line up with nearby inclinations.

Additionally, statistical surveying permits organizations to distinguish holes and neglected needs in the new market. By leading overviews, center gatherings, and investigating existing information, organizations can uncover open doors that may not be quickly evident. This cycle goes past only evaluating the opposition and helps organizations advance and position themselves particularly on the lookout. Recognizing neglected needs gives an establishment to creating items or administrations that satisfy those requirements, giving the business an upper hand.

The serious scene is another basic viewpoint that exhaustive statistical surveying addresses. Understanding who the central members are, their piece of the pie, qualities, and shortcomings permits organizations to plan successful cutthroat methodologies. This examination goes past a superficial comprehension of contenders; it dives into their valuing methodologies, promoting approaches, and consumer loyalty levels. Equipped with this data, organizations can situate themselves decisively, separating their contributions and making a convincing offer for the new market.

Exhaustive statistical surveying additionally gives experiences into the administrative climate of the objective market. Various districts and nations have shifting guidelines and consistence prerequisites that organizations should explore. Understanding these administrative complexities is fundamental to guarantee lawful consistence and stay away from potential legitimate traps that could frustrate market passage. Administrative contemplations can influence item improvement, showcasing informing, and dispersion channels, making it basic for organizations to explore and comprehend the legitimate scene of the new market completely.

Risk relief is a critical target of exhaustive statistical surveying. Each market section implies chances, yet a well-informed procedure permits organizations to distinguish, survey, and moderate these dangers really. Whether it's money gambles, political unsteadiness, or unanticipated social difficulties, organizations can foster alternate courses of action and chance moderation methodologies in light of the experiences acquired from statistical surveying. This proactive methodology upgrades the flexibility of the business and limits the probability of startling difficulties.

The monetary part of market section is a huge thought, and statistical surveying assumes a vital part in monetary preparation. It assists organizations with assessing the potential market size, gauge interest for their items or administrations, and venture income and costs. Precise monetary projections are basic for getting subsidizing, whether through inside assets, outside financial backers, or monetary foundations. Exhaustive statistical surveying gives the information expected to construct practical monetary models that guide planning and speculation choices.

One more significant component of statistical surveying is understanding the appropriation diverts and operations in the new market. Proficient and compelling dispersion is fundamental for arriving at clients and conveying items or administrations as quickly as possibly. Exploring the current circulation foundation, recognizing possible accomplices, and evaluating calculated difficulties assist organizations with smoothing out their inventory network processes and advance dispersion systems for the new market.

Social responsiveness is a variable that can't be disregarded in the worldwide commercial center. Careful statistical surveying permits organizations to acquire social experiences that are essential for fruitful market passage. This incorporates understanding social standards, values, correspondence styles, and cultural perspectives towards specific items or administrations. Social subtleties can fundamentally affect advertising informing, marking, and even item plan, and organizations that disregard these variables might confront difficulties in acquiring acknowledgment and building trust in the new market.

Market division is a vital piece of statistical surveying and helps in focusing on unambiguous client fragments successfully. By recognizing the various fragments inside the new market in view of socioeconomics, psychographics, or conduct, organizations can tailor their showcasing
endeavors to resound with the novel requirements and inclinations of each section. This designated approach builds the pertinence of the business contributions, improves client commitment, and adds to the general progress of market section.

Intensive statistical surveying additionally gives experiences into monetary variables that can impact market section choices. Financial pointers, for example, Gross domestic product development, expansion rates, and pay levels influence shopper buying power and by and large market interest. Understanding the monetary scene assists organizations with surveying the suitability of their estimating procedures, gauge deals potential, and settle on informed conclusions about asset allotment in the new market.

The planning of market passage is a basic thought for organizations, and statistical surveying assumes a vital part in deciding the ideal timing. Timing includes surveying the ongoing economic situations as well as expecting future patterns and improvements. Organizations that enter a market brilliantly can exploit arising valuable open doors and gain a first-mover advantage. Intensive statistical surveying empowers organizations to come to informed conclusions about when to enter another market, considering occasional varieties, financial cycles, and industry patterns.

The advanced time has changed the manner in which organizations direct statistical surveying. Online reviews, virtual entertainment checking, and web examination give constant information and bits of knowledge into customer conduct and opinion. Computerized instruments likewise work with remote exploration, permitting organizations to accumulate data from the objective market without the requirement for an actual presence. The openness and speed of computerized statistical surveying improve its viability in the quick moving worldwide business climate.

Regardless of the upsides of computerized research strategies, organizations should likewise perceive the significance of on-the-ground research, particularly while entering another market with unmistakable social subtleties. In-person meets, center gatherings, and direct perception give subjective bits of knowledge that might be trying to catch through advanced implies alone. Joining computerized devices with customary examination techniques makes an extensive and balanced way to deal with statistical surveying.

Globalization has made the world more interconnected, however it has likewise increased contest. Careful statistical surveying is an essential weapon for organizations meaning to acquire a traction in new business sectors and extend their worldwide presence. Fruitful market passage requires a nuanced comprehension of the worldwide business scene, including international variables, exchange elements, and social variety. Organizations that lead far reaching worldwide statistical surveying can explore the intricacies of global extension all the more successfully.

In rundown, careful statistical surveying is an essential for effective market section. It fills in as the compass that guides organizations through the complexities of another market, assisting them with grasping purchaser inclinations, evaluate rivalry, explore administrative scenes, and relieve gambles. According to a monetary viewpoint, statistical surveying helps with planning and asset portion, while bits of knowledge into conveyance channels, social subtleties, and financial elements add to vital navigation. In a period of quick change and extraordinary worldwide contest, organizations that focus on exhaustive statistical surveying are better situated to go with informed choices that lead to fruitful market passage and supported development.

3.2 Tools and methodologies for market analysis

Devices and systems for market examination have developed essentially with the coming of innovation, giving organizations a different exhibit of instruments to gather important bits of knowledge. In the powerful scene of the present business sectors, remaining ahead requires a comprehension of customary examination techniques as well as a capability in utilizing state of the art devices and systems. From quantitative reviews to cutting edge information examination and man-made reasoning, the apparatuses accessible for market investigation are assorted, empowering organizations to go with informed choices, recognize open doors, and remain receptive to changing buyer ways of behaving.

Quantitative examination techniques are essential devices in market examination, giving mathematical information that can be dissected genuinely. Studies, one of the most widely recognized quantitative examination devices, include gathering organized information through surveys directed to an example of respondents. These reviews can be led through different stations, including on the web stages, phone meetings, or eye to eye collaborations. The organized idea of studies takes into consideration the assortment of normalized information, making it more straightforward to investigate and reach genuinely huge inferences.

Another quantitative examination device is investigations or field preliminaries, where scientists control specific factors and notice their effect available. Controlled tests give significant experiences into circumstances and logical results connections, assisting organizations with understanding how changes in item elements, valuing, or advertising systems impact purchaser conduct. This technique is especially valuable for testing speculations and refining systems before full-scale execution.

Information examination has turned into a unique advantage in market investigation, permitting organizations to extricate significant examples and patterns from enormous datasets. With the ascent of enormous information, organizations can use progressed examination apparatuses to handle immense measures of data and gain experiences that were formerly difficult to acquire.

Distinct investigation, which centers around summing up verifiable information, assists organizations with grasping past patterns. Prescient investigation utilizes factual calculations and AI to conjecture future patterns in light of verifiable information, empowering organizations to expect market moves and pursue proactive choices.

Prescriptive examination makes information investigation a stride further by giving suggestions to activities to streamline results. These high level examination devices enable organizations to settle on information driven choices, whether it's in evaluating techniques, stock administration, or client division. By bridling the force of information examination, organizations can uncover stowed away examples, recognize arising open doors, and refine their market methodologies progressively.

Online entertainment observing apparatuses have become essential for market examination in the advanced age. These devices empower organizations to follow and investigate online discussions, notices, and opinions connected with their image, items, or industry. Virtual entertainment stages act as a tremendous wellspring of unstructured information, and checking instruments use calculations to filter through this information, giving organizations experiences into purchaser conclusions, inclinations, and patterns. Virtual entertainment observing instruments likewise work with contender examination, permitting organizations to keep up to date with industry improvements and feeling shifts.

Web investigation devices are vital for organizations with an internet based presence. These apparatuses track site traffic, client conduct, and commitment measurements, giving significant experiences into the adequacy of internet advertising endeavors. Organizations can investigate information, for example, online visits, bob rates, and change rates to upgrade their sites for better client encounters. Also, web investigation apparatuses offer segment data about site guests, assisting organizations with understanding their internet based crowd and designer content as needs be.

Contender examination devices help organizations in figuring out their cutthroat scene. These apparatuses give information on contenders' piece of the pie, estimating systems, item contributions, and consumer loyalty levels. By benchmarking against contenders, organizations can recognize regions for development, separate their contributions, and foster procedures to acquire an upper hand. Cutthroat investigation instruments range from membership based administrations that give thorough market knowledge to free apparatuses that offer essential experiences.

Client relationship the board (CRM) devices assume a significant part in market examination by bringing together and coordinating client information. These devices track client cooperations, buys, inclinations, and criticism, making a comprehensive perspective on the client venture.

Organizations can utilize CRM information to fragment clients in light of socioeconomics, ways of behaving, or buy history, empowering designated showcasing efforts. CRM devices additionally work with customized correspondence with clients, encouraging more grounded connections and upgrading consumer loyalty.

Geographic data framework (GIS) instruments are significant for organizations with a geographic concentration. These apparatuses utilize spatial information to make guides and representations that assist organizations with understanding the geological dissemination of their objective market. GIS devices can be utilized to break down segment information, distinguish ideal areas for new stores or workplaces, and survey the effect of geographic elements on purchaser conduct. For ventures like retail, land, and operations, GIS instruments give a spatial point of view that illuminates key direction.

AI and man-made brainpower (simulated intelligence) are progressively incorporated into market investigation techniques, offering progressed abilities for information handling and example acknowledgment. AI calculations can examine enormous datasets to recognize patterns, anticipate buyer conduct, and mechanize dynamic cycles. Artificial intelligence controlled chatbots and remote helpers improve client cooperations, giving organizations constant bits of knowledge into client questions and concerns. The utilization of artificial intelligence in market examination keeps on developing, with applications going from interest determining to feeling investigation.

Online reviews and criticism devices have become instrumental in gathering continuous suppositions and inclinations from shoppers. These devices permit organizations to make and disperse overviews proficiently, contacting a wide crowd across different socioeconomics. Online overview stages frequently give adaptable formats, investigation dashboards, and feeling examination highlights, smoothing out the information assortment and investigation process. Organizations can utilize online reviews to assemble criticism on items, measure consumer loyalty, and recognize regions for development.

Center gatherings stay a subjective examination strategy that supplements quantitative methodologies by giving inside and out experiences into customer discernments and perspectives. While customary center gatherings include eye to eye communications, virtual center gatherings have acquired ubiquity, permitting members to draw in from various areas. Center gatherings are especially helpful for investigating nuanced parts of buyer conduct, acquiring subjective input on new item ideas, and revealing insights that may not be caught through quantitative reviews alone.

Ethnographic examination includes the vivid investigation of buyers in their regular habitats. Specialists notice and collaborate with shoppers, all things considered, settings to acquire a profound comprehension of their ways of behaving, inclinations, and dynamic cycles.

Ethnographic examination goes past what customers say in reviews or center gatherings, giving organizations bits of knowledge into the setting of buyer encounters. This strategy is especially applicable for businesses where noticing purchaser conduct in genuine settings is critical, like retail or neighborliness.

Powerhouse showcasing devices help organizations in distinguishing and working together with forces to be reckoned with who can enhance their image reach. These devices examine online entertainment measurements, commitment levels, and crowd socioeconomics to evaluate the impact of likely colleagues. Organizations can utilize powerhouse advertising instruments to find powerhouses lined up with their image values and interest group. By utilizing powerhouses, organizations can take advantage of laid out networks, fabricate brand mindfulness, and upgrade validity.

SWOT examination stays a crucial strategy for evaluating the inward qualities and shortcomings of a business, alongside outer open doors and dangers on the lookout. By deliberately assessing these variables, organizations can foster an essential comprehension of their cutthroat position. SWOT examination is in many cases utilized related to different devices and techniques, giving a thorough structure to vital preparation and direction.

Situation arranging is a forward-looking technique that includes investigating various future situations and evaluating their likely effect on the business. This apparatus assists organizations with expecting vulnerabilities, distinguish likely dangers, and foster alternate courses of action. Situation arranging is especially important in unpredictable business sectors or enterprises going through quick change, giving organizations an essential prescience that illuminates direction and hazard the board.

Client personas are fictitious portrayals of ideal clients in view of segment, psychographic, and social information. Organizations make client personas to refine their interest group and designer showcasing systems to explicit portions. Client personas assist organizations with figuring out the inspirations, inclinations, and problem areas of their clients, directing the improvement of items, administrations, and advertising messages that resound with the target group.

Benchmarking is a relative examination device that includes considering a business' presentation in contrast to industry guidelines or contenders. By distinguishing key execution pointers (KPIs) and contrasting them and benchmarks, organizations gain experiences into their general assets and regions for development. Benchmarking is a continuous cycle that illuminates consistent improvement endeavors, assisting organizations with remaining serious and receptive to advertise changes.

Net Advertiser Score (NPS) is a broadly involved measurement for estimating consumer loyalty and reliability. NPS is gotten from a straightforward study question that asks clients that they are so prone to prescribe an item or administration to other people.

Respondents are arranged as advertisers, passives, or doubters in view of their reactions. NPS gives a quantifiable proportion of client devotion, with high NPS scores showing fulfilled clients liable to advance the brand.

A/B testing, otherwise called split testing, is a strategy for looking at two variants of a page, email, or showcasing message to figure out which performs better. By haphazardly relegating various variants to an example of clients, organizations can investigate the exhibition measurements and distinguish the rendition that yields improved results. A/B testing is important for streamlining web composition, showcasing efforts, and other client confronting components.

Relapse examination is a measurable procedure that looks at the connection among reliant and free factors. In market examination, relapse investigation assists organizations with understanding the elements impacting specific results, like deals or consumer loyalty. By distinguishing connections and evaluating the strength of connections, organizations can put forth information driven choices and focus on attempts in light of elements that altogether influence their targets.

Game hypothesis, albeit customarily connected with financial aspects, is progressively applied in market examination to display vital associations between contenders. Organizations utilize game hypothesis to expect contenders' moves, evaluate possible results of key choices, and plan ideal techniques in cutthroat conditions. Game hypothesis gives a hypothetical structure to grasping the elements of rivalry and participation in business sectors.

Choice trees are visual portrayals that assist organizations with breaking down dynamic cycles and possible results. In market examination, choice trees can be utilized to demonstrate various situations, evaluate the likelihood of every result, and distinguish the most great choices. This procedure is especially valuable for organizations confronting complex choices with numerous factors and possible results.

These instruments and techniques on the whole add to a powerful and complex way to deal with market examination. The selection of apparatuses relies upon the particular targets of the investigation, the idea of the market, and the accessible assets. Organizations that influence a mix of customary and high level devices are better prepared to explore the intricacies of the present business sectors, pursue informed choices, and remain spry notwithstanding developing purchaser ways of behaving and market elements.

3.3 Studies illustrating successful and unsuccessful market entries

Looking at contextual analyses that represent both effective and fruitless market passages gives important bits of knowledge into the elements that add to wins or disappointments in the mind boggling field of worldwide business. Gaining from the encounters of different organizations clarifies the basic choices, procedures, and traps that can essentially influence the result of a market section. By diving into these genuine models, organizations can determine significant examples and apply them to their own market passage attempts, improving the probability of progress while keeping away from normal traps.

One striking instance of an effective market passage is the extension of Starbucks into China. Starbucks, the American café chain, left on its global excursion with a wary and key methodology. China, with its huge populace and arising working class, addressed a rewarding business sector opportunity. In any case, Starbucks perceived the need to adjust its contributions to suit the nearby taste inclinations and social subtleties.

In the mid 2000s, Starbucks confronted beginning difficulties in China, where tea-drinking customs won, and the espresso culture was not quite so profoundly imbued as in Western nations. The organization changed its methodology by presenting refreshments that mixed espresso with customary Chinese fixings, for example, green tea lattes and red bean frappuccinos. Furthermore, Starbucks made a warm and welcoming feel in its stores, giving a space to mingling and conferences, which resounded with the Chinese purchaser way of life.

Starbucks put vigorously in understanding the neighborhood market, leading careful statistical surveying, and building associations with nearby accomplices. Teaming up with neighborhood organizations explored administrative necessities and gain social experiences. The organization's obligation to restriction, joined with its superior image picture, added to its outcome in China. Starbucks is currently one of the main espresso chains in the nation, showing the way that adjusting to nearby inclinations and building solid connections can prompt an effective market passage.

Running against the norm, the instance of eBay's fruitless section into China fills in as a wake up call. In the mid 2000s, eBay, the worldwide web based business goliath, confronted difficulties in acquiring a traction in the Chinese market, which was overwhelmed by nearby contenders. One of the basic mix-ups made by eBay was its misjudgement of the interesting attributes of the Chinese internet business scene and purchaser conduct.

Neighborhood contenders, like Alibaba's Taobao, offered free postings and stressed a buyer to-purchaser (C2C) model, though eBay at first depended on a business-to-customer (B2C) model with exchange charges. The inclination with the expectation of complimentary postings and the emphasis on C2C exchanges were more lined up with the Chinese shopper outlook.

Furthermore, eBay's choice to charge exchange expenses and its hesitance to take on a neighborhood installment framework presented difficulties in a market where shoppers were familiar with free administrations and favored utilizing nearby installment strategies.

Besides, eBay confronted hardships in building trust among Chinese buyers. Fake and bad quality items were common on the stage, subverting the dependability of the commercial center. Nearby contenders, for example, Taobao, addressed this worry by executing measures to guarantee item realness and quality. eBay attempted to lay out serious areas of strength for a presence and neglected to adjust its system to the interesting elements of the Chinese online business market.

The instance of eBay features the significance of understanding and adjusting to neighborhood economic situations. Ignoring social inclinations, underrating the meaning of trust, and neglecting to line up with winning plans of action can prompt market passage disappointments. This case underlines the requirement for organizations to direct exhaustive statistical surveying, tailor their methodologies to nearby buyer ways of behaving, and focus on building trust in new business sectors.

One more critical illustration of an effective market section is the extension of IKEA into the Indian market. IKEA, the Swedish global furniture retailer, confronted the test of entering a market with different purchaser inclinations, particular social contemplations, and a complex administrative climate. In any case, IKEA's careful way to deal with grasping the neighborhood scene and adjusting its plan of action added to its outcome in India.

IKEA perceived the significance of moderateness in the Indian market and changed its item contributions and valuing techniques likewise. The organization presented a scope of items custom fitted to Indian preferences and inclinations, integrating components of Indian plan and craftsmanship. IKEA likewise went with key choices to restrict its production network, obtaining materials locally to lessen expenses and improve productivity.

Understanding the meaning of the home and family in Indian culture, IKEA made vivid in-store encounters that displayed the usefulness and plan of its furniture, in actuality, settings. The organization put resources into understanding the nearby production network, dispersion organizations, and administrative prerequisites to guarantee a consistent and savvy activity in India.

IKEA's progress in India represents the significance of variation and limitation. By integrating nearby components into its item contributions, changing evaluating techniques, and putting resources into a vivid retail insight, IKEA showed a guarantee to understanding and meeting the remarkable requirements of the Indian customer. This case highlights the significance of adaptability and social awareness in making progress in assorted markets.

On the other hand, the instance of Walmart's ineffective section into Germany features the difficulties that can emerge when an organization neglects to adjust its plan of action to neighborhood conditions. In the mid 2000s, Walmart, the American retail monster, confronted hardships in building up some forward movement in the German market, at last prompting its choice to leave the market.

Walmart entered Germany through the procurement of the neighborhood corporate store Wertkauf and the hypermarket chain Interspar. In any case, the organization battled with social contrasts, strategic difficulties, and an absence of comprehension of the German shopper mentality. Walmart's obligation to its minimal expense model, portrayed by enormous stores and broad item varieties, didn't reverberate with German purchasers who favored more modest, more particular stores.

Calculated shortcomings likewise assumed a part in Walmart's difficulties in Germany. The organization's dependence on a unified circulation framework, normal in the US, ended up being less viable in Germany's decentralized market. Walmart confronted hardships in overseeing stock, guaranteeing ideal restocking, and adjusting to the inclinations of German buyers.

Additionally, Walmart's correspondence and showcasing procedures didn't line up with the assumptions for German buyers. The organization's accentuation on regular low costs and cost reserve funds didn't reverberate in a market where customers put a higher worth on quality and administration. Walmart's inability to perceive and adjust to these social subtleties added to its failure to acquire a cutthroat traction in Germany.

The instance of Walmart in Germany highlights the significance of understanding and adjusting to neighborhood inclinations and market structures. It features the requirement for adaptability in plans of action, production network the board, and advertising methodologies while entering different business sectors. Walmart's involvement with Germany fills in as a preventative model, underlining that progress in one market doesn't ensure outcome in another, requiring a nuanced and socially delicate way to deal with market passage.

A differentiating instance of effective market passage is the extension of Apple Inc. into China. Apple's entrance into the Chinese market has been set apart by essential choices that line up with the one of a kind elements of the country's customer hardware scene. Apple perceived the capability of the huge Chinese market and decisively situated itself as a superior brand taking care of the developing center and upper-working class sections.

Apple's progress in China can be credited to a few elements, remembering its concentration for item development, brand picture, and vital organizations. The organization presented lead items like the iPhone, iPad, and MacBook, which engaged Chinese shoppers looking for superior grade, optimistic items.

Apple's accentuation on plan, client experience, and state of the art innovation reverberated with the inclinations of Chinese customers who esteem premium brands.

Vital associations with neighborhood transporters and retailers worked with Apple's dissemination and market arrive at in China. Working together with neighborhood accomplices explored administrative prerequisites, lay out areas of strength for a presence, and make custom-made showcasing efforts. Apple's obligation to client care and building an optimistic brand picture added to the progress of its market passage in China.

Nonetheless, not all innovation organizations have encountered progress in China. Google's entrance into the Chinese web crawler market fills in as an instance of a fruitless market passage. During the 2000s, Google entered China with an edited form of its web crawler to follow the country's web oversight guidelines. In spite of starting development, Google confronted difficulties connected with control, rivalry, and network safety concerns.

In 2010, Google chose to leave the Chinese web search tool market, refering to worries about restriction and digital assaults. The choice to pull out was additionally impacted by expanding contest from neighborhood web search tools and the difficulties of working inside the bounds of China's administrative climate. Google's exit from China denoted a mishap in its worldwide development technique and featured the intricacies of exploring the Chinese market.

The instance of Google in China highlights the significance of understanding and exploring administrative difficulties in unfamiliar business sectors. It additionally stresses the requirement for organizations to consider the moral ramifications of their business choices, particularly in business sectors with extraordinary administrative necessities cautiously. Google's involvement with China fills in as an update that consistence with nearby guidelines, social responsive qualities, and moral contemplations is fundamental for supported outcome in worldwide business sectors.

A case showing fruitful market passage in the drug business is that of Pfizer in India. Pfizer, a main worldwide drug organization, decisively entered the Indian market through a blend of acquisitions and coordinated efforts. Perceiving the capability of India as a critical market for drugs, Pfizer did whatever it may take to lay out major areas of strength for some time adjusting to the nearby medical services scene.

Pfizer's securing of Pharmacia in 2003 and Wyeth in 2009 reinforced its item portfolio and piece of the pie in India. The organization likewise went into vital joint efforts with Indian drug organizations, utilizing neighborhood skill and assets. Pfizer's emphasis on remedial regions with high predominance in India, like cardiovascular sicknesses and diabetes, lined up with the country's medical services needs.

Furthermore, Pfizer focused on innovative work exercises in India, adding to the nearby drug environment. The organization's obligation to quality, consistence with administrative norms, and commitment with medical services experts assisted form with trusting among Indian buyers and medical services specialists. Pfizer's outcome in India represents the significance of key organizations, portfolio improvement, and a patient-driven approach in the drug area.

Interestingly, the instance of Nokia's ineffective market passage into the cell phone industry fills in as a useful example of a once-predominant player neglecting to adjust to changing business sector elements. Nokia, a Finnish media communications and purchaser hardware organization, confronted difficulties in the change from highlight telephones to cell phones. The development of contenders like Apple's iPhone and Android-based gadgets upset Nokia's predominance in the cell phone market.

Nokia's inability to rapidly take on touchscreen innovation, embrace an easy to understand working framework, and enhance in the cell phone space added to its decay. The organization's perseverance in advancing its Symbian working framework while contenders embraced more natural stages hampered its seriousness. Also, Nokia's deferred passage into the application environment further reduced appeal to customers were progressively focusing on application rich cell phones.

The instance of Nokia highlights the significance of advancement, versatility, and remaining receptive to purchaser inclinations in the innovation area. The fast development of the cell phone market showed the way that even settled pioneers can confront difficulties assuming they neglect to embrace extraordinary advances and adjust to changing customer assumptions. Nokia's experience fills in as a suggestion to organizations to stay spry, put resources into development, and expect shifts in the serious scene.

A case exhibiting fruitful market passage in the cheap food industry is that of McDonald's in Japan. Mcdonald's, the worldwide cheap food monster, entered the Japanese market in 1971, and its prosperity can be credited to a blend of confinement, transformation, and comprehension of the nearby culture. Perceiving the novel inclinations of Japanese shoppers, McDonald's custom fitted its menu, showcasing methodologies, and store plans to suit the nearby setting.

McDonald's presented things, for example, the Teriyaki Burger and the Shrimp Burger to take care of Japanese taste inclinations. The organization additionally stressed tidiness, productivity, and client assistance, lining up with social qualities in Japan. McDonald's put resources into store plans that gave an agreeable and family-accommodating climate, reverberating with the Japanese accentuation on bunch feasting and family trips.

Vital organizations with nearby providers guaranteed a steady production network and added to the limitation endeavors. McDonald's outcome in Japan represents the significance of social transformation, menu confinement, and a profound comprehension of nearby customer conduct in the food and drink industry.

EXPORT STRATEGIES

Conversely, the instance of Home Terminal's fruitless market section into China features the difficulties of moving an effective plan of action starting with one market then onto the next without adequate variation. Home Warehouse, a main American home improvement retailer, entered China in 2006 with exclusive standards however confronted hardships in getting momentum.

Home Stop's accentuation on DIY (Do-It-Yourself) culture, a fruitful part of its plan of action in the US, didn't line up with the predominant practices in the Chinese home improvement market. Chinese shoppers regularly depended on proficient workers for hire for home improvement projects, and the Do-It-Yourself approach was not as common. Home Station's enormous store designs and broad item varieties likewise introduced difficulties in a market where space constraints and confined needs were critical elements.

Besides, Home Stop confronted contest from nearby retailers with a superior comprehension of the Chinese market. The organization attempted to separate itself and neglected to catch a critical piece of the pie. In 2012, Home Terminal reported its choice to shut down its leftover stores in China, denoting a fruitless endeavor into the Chinese home improvement market.

The instance of Home Terminal in China highlights the significance of adjusting plans of action to neighborhood market elements and customer ways of behaving. It features the requirement for organizations to direct intensive statistical surveying, grasp social subtleties, and designer their procedures to line up with neighborhood inclinations. Home Stop's experience fills in as an update that outcome in one market doesn't ensure progress in another, underscoring the significance of vital limitation in worldwide developments.

Chapter 4

Developing a Robust Export Plan

Fostering a vigorous commodity plan is a basic endeavor for organizations looking to extend their market reach and benefit from worldwide open doors. A viable commodity plan fills in as a guide, directing organizations through the intricacies of worldwide exchange, administrative consistence, and social subtleties. Whether entering new business sectors or extending existing ones, organizations should make a well-informed and vital product intend to explore the difficulties and profit by the possible compensations of worldwide exchange.

Statistical surveying and Choice:

The underpinning of a powerful product plan lies in far reaching statistical surveying and choice. Distinguishing objective business sectors includes assessing variables, for example, market size, development potential, rivalry, and administrative conditions. Careful exploration assists organizations with grasping buyer ways of behaving, inclinations, and social subtleties in the objective business sectors. Also, surveying the monetary and political strength of potential business sectors is vital for risk the executives.

Item Variation and Situating:

Fruitful global development expects organizations to fit their items or administrations to meet the particular requirements and inclinations of target markets. Item transformation might include adjusting highlights, bundling, or estimating to line up with neighborhood assumptions. Creating a convincing incentive that reverberates with the objective market is fundamental for powerful situating. Understanding how the item squeezes into the nearby serious scene is basic for acquiring an upper hand.

Legitimate and Administrative Consistence:

Exploring the legitimate and administrative scene is a central part of fostering a product plan. Various nations have shifting guidelines overseeing imports, customs strategies, and item norms. Organizations should direct an intensive survey of commodity controls, taxes, and economic deals relevant to their objective business sectors.

Consistence with worldwide exchange regulations and adherence to quality guidelines are basic to stay away from legitimate entanglements and guarantee smooth cross-line exchanges.

Dissemination Channels and Coordinated operations:

Choosing the right dissemination channels and laying out proficient strategies are key parts of a hearty commodity plan. Organizations need to choose whether to work with wholesalers, specialists, or lay out their own presence in the objective market.

Assessing transportation, warehousing, and satisfaction choices streamlines production network proficiency. A powerful coordinated operations procedure guarantees opportune conveyance, diminishes expenses, and upgrades consumer loyalty, adding to long haul progress in global business sectors.

Monetary Preparation and Chance Administration:

Monetary arranging is a significant part of any product plan. Organizations should assess the expenses related with send out exercises, including creation, transportation, levies, and promoting. Making nitty gritty monetary projections helps in planning and asset designation. Furthermore, fostering a gamble the executives procedure is fundamental to relieve potential difficulties like cash variances, political flimsiness, and changes in economic situations. Using monetary instruments, such as supporting, can help safeguard against money chances.

Market Section Methodology:

Choosing the right market section methodology is a crucial choice in the product arranging process. Choices range from direct products to laying out joint endeavors or associations with neighborhood substances. The decision of section technique relies upon variables like market attributes, administrative necessities, and the degree of control the business looks for. For certain organizations, a progressive methodology, like beginning with backhanded sends out through middle people, might be a reasonable technique prior to focusing on additional significant ventures.

Social and Correspondence Contemplations:

Compelling correspondence and social awareness are fundamental to effective worldwide undertakings. Organizations need to adjust their showcasing messages, marking, and correspondence styles to reverberate with the social standards and upsides of the objective market. Utilizing nearby language in advertising materials and understanding social subtleties assists fabricate trust and encourages positive associations with clients and accomplices.

Market Entrance and Advancement:

Fostering a vigorous showcasing and advancement methodology is fundamental for market infiltration. Organizations ought to use a blend of customary and computerized showcasing channels to make mindfulness and create interest in their items or administrations. Fitting showcasing efforts to nearby inclinations and ways of behaving upgrades their viability. Taking part in special exercises, partaking in career expos, and utilizing web-based entertainment stages add to building serious areas of strength for a presence.

Monetary Help and Government Backing:

Numerous state run administrations give monetary help, motivations, and backing projects to urge organizations to participate in worldwide exchange. Organizations ought to investigate accessible assets, for example, send out funding projects, awards, or protection plans.

Working together with government organizations that advance commodities can give important experiences, organizing open doors, and monetary help. Exploiting these assets fortifies the monetary underpinning of the product plan.

Preparing and Limit Building:

Getting ready workers and partners for worldwide exchange is pivotal for the effective execution of a commodity plan. Preparing projects ought to cover viewpoints like culturally diverse correspondence, global exchange guidelines, and market-explicit information. Building the limit of the labor force improves their capacity to explore the intricacies of worldwide business and adds to the general progress of the commodity adventure.

Checking and Assessment:

A vigorous commodity plan incorporates components for constant observing and assessment. Organizations ought to lay out key execution pointers (KPIs) to survey the adequacy of the commodity procedure. Consistently investigating deals execution, client criticism, and market elements distinguishes regions for development and illuminates vital changes. Adaptability and responsiveness to changing economic situations are fundamental for long haul achievement.

Contextual investigations Delineating Effective Commodity Plans:

Looking at contextual investigations of organizations that have effectively executed trade plans gives important experiences into viable systems and best practices. One such case is the development of the auto organization Tesla into worldwide business sectors. Tesla's essential methodology included laying out a worldwide store network, adjusting its electric vehicles to meet nearby guidelines, and putting resources into charging foundation. The organization's emphasis on advancement, economical practices, and understanding different buyer inclinations added to its fruitful worldwide extension.

One more critical case is the worldwide development of the internet business goliath Amazon. Amazon's product achievement can be ascribed to its strong operations framework, easy to use stage, and versatile way to deal with nearby business sectors. By modifying its contributions, exploring administrative scenes, and building solid organizations, Amazon has turned into a worldwide commercial center with a huge presence in different nations. The organization's obligation to consumer loyalty, effective conveyance, and constant development has been instrumental in its global achievement.

EXPORT STRATEGIES

Difficulties and Illustrations Gained from Fruitless Product Plans:

Understanding the difficulties looked by organizations with ineffective product plans is similarly significant for inferring important illustrations. One such case is the battles experienced by the American retailer Walmart in its venture into the German market. Walmart's difficulties included social contrasts, an absence of comprehension of German shopping propensities, and inflexible adherence to its minimal expense model.

The organization's inability to adjust to neighborhood inclinations and contest brought about a huge difficulty, stressing the significance of social responsiveness and market transformation.

Also, the instance of the refreshment organization Coca-Cola's bombed endeavor to present its Dasani filtered water in the UK features the meaning of grasping neighborhood customer discernments. Dasani confronted negative exposure because of the disclosure that the item was obtained from faucet water and went through a cleansing interaction. The absence of social mindfulness with respect to shopper perspectives toward filtered water and the oversight in promoting added to the item's disappointment in the UK market. This case highlights the significance of intensive statistical surveying and adjusting items to neighborhood shopper assumptions.

4.1 Crafting a comprehensive export plan

Making an extensive product plan is an essential basic for organizations trying to wander into global business sectors. A commodity plan fills in as a guide, illustrating the means and procedures important to explore the intricacies of worldwide exchange effectively. It includes fastidious exploration, cautious preparation, and a profound comprehension of the objective business sectors to guarantee that organizations can gain by open doors while successfully relieving chances. In this extensive product plan, we will dive into the critical parts and contemplations that organizations ought to address to figure out a strong system for worldwide development.

Statistical surveying and Determination:

The groundwork of an effective commodity plan lies in careful statistical surveying and the essential determination of target markets. Organizations need to break down potential business sectors in view of measures, for example, market size, development possibilities, contest, and administrative conditions. Figuring out the social subtleties, buyer ways of behaving, and inclinations in the picked markets is essential for fitting items or administrations to fulfill nearby need. Statistical surveying gives the fundamental foundation to pursuing informed choices and alleviating gambles related with entering new domains.

Item Variation and Situating:

Adjusting items or administrations to meet the exceptional necessities and inclinations of target markets is a basic move toward making a commodity plan. Item transformation includes surveying whether alterations to elements, bundling, or estimating are important to line up with nearby assumptions. Making a convincing incentive that reverberates with the objective market improves the situating of the item. Effective item transformation guarantees that organizations are offering arrangements that are socially important as well as seriously situated in the neighborhood market.

Lawful and Administrative Consistence:

Exploring the lawful and administrative scene is an essential part of any product plan. Various nations have fluctuating guidelines overseeing imports, customs systems, and item norms. Organizations should direct an intensive survey of commodity controls, taxes, and economic deals pertinent to their objective business sectors. Consistence with global exchange regulations and adherence to quality norms are basic to stay away from legitimate difficulties and guarantee smooth cross-line exchanges.

Dispersion Channels and Strategies:

Picking the right dispersion channels and laying out effective strategies are essential parts of an exhaustive commodity plan. Organizations need to choose whether to work with merchants, specialists, or lay out their own presence in the objective market. Assessing transportation, warehousing, and satisfaction choices advances the store network for opportune conveyance, decreased costs, and improved consumer loyalty. A powerful operations system guarantees that items arrive at the end buyer in a convenient and practical way.

Monetary Preparation and Hazard The executives:

Monetary arranging is a pivotal part of a commodity plan, incorporating cost assessments, planning, and asset designation. Organizations should expect the expenses related with trade exercises, including creation, transportation, levies, and promoting. Creating itemized monetary projections helps with monetary preparation and chance relief. Furthermore, laying out a gamble the board procedure is fundamental to relieve difficulties like cash vacillations, political shakiness, and changes in economic situations. Using monetary instruments, such as supporting, can help safeguard against cash chances.

Market Passage Technique:

The fact that shapes the product plan makes picking a fitting business sector passage technique a crucial choice. Market passage choices range from direct products to laying out joint endeavors or associations with nearby substances. The decision of passage procedure relies upon elements like market attributes, administrative necessities, and the degree of control the business looks for. A very much created passage procedure lines up with the general business targets and lays the basis for fruitful market entrance.

Social and Correspondence Contemplations:

Viable correspondence and social awareness are fundamental to the outcome of a product plan. Organizations should adjust their showcasing messages, marking, and correspondence styles to resound with the social standards and upsides of the objective market. Utilizing nearby language in showcasing materials and understanding social subtleties assist assemble trust and cultivate positive associations with clients and accomplices. Social mindfulness adds to fruitful market situating and assists organizations with keeping away from correspondence traps that might emerge from social contrasts.

Market Entrance and Advancement:
Fostering a powerful showcasing and advancement technique is fundamental for fruitful market entrance. Organizations ought to use a blend of customary and computerized promoting channels to make mindfulness and create interest in their items or administrations. Fitting showcasing efforts to nearby inclinations and ways of behaving improves their viability. Participating in special exercises, taking part in career expos, and utilizing virtual entertainment stages add to building major areas of strength for a presence.

Monetary Help and Government Backing:
Numerous states give monetary help, motivating forces, and backing projects to urge organizations to take part in global exchange. Investigating accessible assets, for example, send out funding projects, awards, or protection plans, can furnish organizations with monetary help. Working together with government organizations that advance products can offer important experiences, organizing potential open doors, and backing in exploring administrative intricacies. Utilizing these assets fortifies the monetary underpinning of the commodity plan.

Preparing and Limit Building:
Getting ready workers and partners for worldwide exchange is significant for the effective execution of a commodity plan. Preparing projects ought to cover perspectives like multifaceted correspondence, worldwide exchange guidelines, and market-explicit information. Building the limit of the labor force improves their capacity to explore the intricacies of worldwide business and adds to the general progress of the commodity adventure.

Checking and Assessment:
A far reaching send out plan incorporates components for persistent observing and assessment. Laying out key execution pointers (KPIs) surveys the adequacy of the commodity system. Consistently checking on deals execution, client criticism, and market elements distinguishes regions for development and illuminates key changes. Adaptability and responsiveness to changing economic situations are fundamental for long haul progress in worldwide business sectors.

Contextual investigations Outlining Effective Product Plans:
Looking at contextual investigations of organizations that have effectively carried out send out plans gives important bits of knowledge into viable procedures and best practices. One such case is the development of the innovation organization Apple Inc. into global business sectors. Apple's essential methodology included laying out a worldwide store network, adjusting its items to meet neighborhood guidelines, and putting resources into limited showcasing. The organization's emphasis on

development, client experience, and a top notch brand picture added to its fruitful worldwide extension.

One more essential case is the worldwide extension of the inexpensive food monster Mcdonald's. McDonald's prosperity can be ascribed to its strong establishment model, limited menu contributions, and versatile way to deal with neighborhood markets. By understanding social inclinations and fitting its menu to meet neighborhood tastes, McDonald's has turned into a worldwide brand with a critical presence in different nations. The organization's obligation to consistency in quality and brand situating has been instrumental in its worldwide achievement.

Difficulties and Examples Gained from Fruitless Product Plans:

Understanding the difficulties looked by organizations with ineffective commodity plans is similarly significant for determining important illustrations. One such case is the battles experienced by the American retailer Focus in its venture into the Canadian market. Target confronted difficulties connected with store network issues, stock administration, and an absence of comprehension of Canadian purchaser inclinations. The organization's inability to adjust to nearby market elements and meet client assumptions brought about a huge mishap, underlining the significance of statistical surveying and transformation.

Also, the instance of the dress retailer Hole's fruitless passage into the Indian market features the difficulties of social variation and grasping nearby purchaser inclinations. Hole confronted hardships in reverberating with Indian shoppers because of its estimating procedure, item situating, and absence of mindfulness about the neighborhood market. The case highlights the significance of adjusting items to nearby assumptions, estimating techniques, and social aversions to prevail in different business sectors.

4.2 Setting clear objectives and goals for international expansion

Laying out clear targets and objectives for worldwide development is a central stage in the essential arranging process for organizations looking to develop their worldwide impression. Clear cut targets act as core values, giving concentration and course to the whole worldwide development exertion. Whether an organization is entering new business sectors, extending existing ones, or broadening its item contributions, laying out clear and quantifiable objectives is significant for progress. In this thorough investigation, we will dig into the vital contemplations and parts engaged with laying out targets and objectives for global development.

Understanding the Business Scene:

Prior to setting targets for worldwide development, organizations should direct an exhaustive examination of the worldwide business scene. This incorporates evaluating the monetary circumstances, market patterns, and international factors that might influence the outcome of worldwide undertakings. A thorough comprehension of the objective business sectors, including social subtleties, administrative conditions, and serious scenes, frames the reason for setting sensible and reachable targets.

Characterizing Key Goal:

Key goal embodies the general reason and course of global development. It includes characterizing why the business is looking for worldwide development, what it plans to accomplish, and how it expects to situate itself in the worldwide commercial center. Key expectation goes past monetary measurements and includes more extensive desires like market administration, memorability, and commitments to neighborhood networks. Clear essential expectation gives a binding together vision that adjusts all parts of the business to its global objectives.

Market Section Goals:

For organizations entering new business sectors, characterizing explicit market passage goals is vital. This might include putting forth objectives connected with portion of the overall industry, client procurement, or geographic extension. Goals ought to be custom-made to the attributes of the objective market, taking into account factors, for example, market size, development potential, and serious elements. Market passage targets give a system to molding market section techniques and deciding the degree of input required.

Item or Administration Development Objectives:

Assuming that the objective of worldwide development includes acquainting new items or administrations with existing business sectors, organizations need to verbalize clear item extension objectives. These objectives might spin around expanding the item portfolio, catching extra market fragments, or answering developing client needs. The targets ought to be lined up with the business' general item advancement and development methodologies, guaranteeing that worldwide extension adds to the expansion and development of the item or administration contributions.

Monetary Targets:

Monetary goals are integral to worldwide extension and incorporate a scope of measurements, including income targets, net revenues, and profit from speculation (return on initial capital investment). Organizations should lay out sensible monetary objectives that mirror the venture expected for global exercises and the expected returns. These targets give a quantitative premise to estimating the progress of worldwide development endeavors and directing monetary preparation and asset designation.

Risk Moderation Objectives:

Global development innately implies gambles, going from money variances to international vulnerabilities. Laying out objectives connected with risk alleviation is fundamental for guaranteeing the strength of the extension procedure. Organizations ought to explain targets around overseeing and limiting dangers, whether through viable supporting systems, possibility arranging, or complete gamble evaluations. The capacity to proactively address difficulties adds to the manageability of worldwide tasks.

Social and Brand Goals:

Social variation and brand situating are basic parts of global development. Organizations ought to set goals connected with social combination, guaranteeing that items, showcasing messages, and strategic policies line up with neighborhood customs and values. Simultaneously, characterizing brand-related objectives, for example, laying out serious areas of strength for a presence, improving brand mindfulness, and building brand steadfastness, adds to effective market passage and supported development.

Innovation and Advancement Objectives:

In an undeniably interconnected worldwide scene, utilizing innovation and cultivating advancement are key drivers of global achievement. Setting targets connected with mechanical headways and development assists organizations with remaining cutthroat and receptive to showcase changes. Objectives might incorporate the reception of cutting edge innovations, the improvement of inventive items or administrations, or the foundation of associations to upgrade mechanical abilities.

Supportability and Corporate Social Obligation (CSR) Goals:

Integrating supportability and CSR targets into global extension objectives mirrors the developing significance of mindful strategic policies. Putting forth objectives connected with ecological supportability, moral obtaining, and local area commitment exhibits a guarantee to social obligation. Adjusting worldwide development to maintainable and moral practices improves brand notoriety as well as adds to long haul business practicality.

Ability and Human Asset Objectives:

Global extension frequently requires an assorted and talented labor force fit for exploring various business sectors. Setting targets connected with ability obtaining, preparing, and improvement guarantees that the business has the human resources important for fruitful worldwide tasks. Objectives might incorporate structure multifaceted skills among representatives, laying out global ability pipelines, and cultivating a different and comprehensive work environment culture.

Legitimate and Consistence Targets:

Exploring complex worldwide legitimate and administrative scenes is a basic part of effective worldwide extension. Setting targets connected with legitimate consistence, risk the board, and administrative adherence mitigates lawful difficulties. Organizations ought to lay out objectives for understanding and following neighborhood regulations, exchange guidelines, and industry-explicit necessities to keep away from lawful inconveniences that might obstruct worldwide activities.

Key Organizations and Collusions:

Coordinated effort through essential organizations and collusions can be instrumental in global development.

Setting goals connected with recognizing and shaping key organizations assists organizations with taking advantage of neighborhood mastery, access conveyance organizations, and improve market validity. Objectives might incorporate laying out collusions with neighborhood organizations, entering joint endeavors, or shaping coordinated efforts with industry pioneers to reinforce market presence.

Government and Exchange Relations Objectives:

Drawing in with government substances and building positive exchange relations is fundamental for exploring the administrative scene and getting to help programs. Setting goals connected with government relations includes laying out a useful discourse with significant specialists, taking part in exchange affiliations, and utilizing discretionary channels. These objectives add to establishing an empowering climate for worldwide development and tending to expected administrative difficulties.

Key Execution Pointers (KPIs):

To quantify progress toward global extension objectives, organizations should distinguish and follow key execution markers (KPIs). These measurements ought to line up with the particular targets set for every feature of the development technique. Whether estimating monetary execution, portion of the overall industry, consumer loyalty, or maintainability measurements, KPIs give quantifiable benchmarks to assessing achievement and illuminating key changes.

Situation Arranging and Adaptability:

While setting targets is critical, organizations should likewise integrate situation arranging and adaptability into their worldwide development procedure. The worldwide business scene is dynamic, and unanticipated difficulties might emerge. Targets ought to be joined by alternate courses of action and the adaptability to adjust systems in light of changing economic situations, international occasions, or changes in purchaser conduct.

Contextual investigations Representing Fruitful Goal Setting:

Inspecting contextual analyses of organizations that have effectively set and accomplished worldwide extension targets gives significant bits of knowledge into successful methodologies. One such case is the development of the innovation monster Google. Google's essential goal was to lay out a worldwide presence as the main web search tool and internet publicizing stage. The organization put forth clear objectives connected with piece of the pie, client commitment, and income age. Through nonstop development, vital acquisitions, and an emphasis on client experience, Google accomplished its targets and turned into a predominant player in the worldwide tech industry.

One more eminent case is the global extension of the inexpensive food chain Mcdonald's. McDonald's set goals centered around adjusting its menu to neighborhood tastes, laying out major areas of strength for a presence, and making normalized functional cycles.

The organization's objectives were lined up with its obligation to giving steady quality and a natural feasting experience across different societies. McDonald's progress in accomplishing these targets is apparent in its far and wide worldwide presence and social versatility.

Difficulties and Examples Gained from Ineffective Goal Setting:

Understanding the difficulties looked by organizations with fruitless global extension goals is similarly significant for determining important examples. One such case is the battles experienced by the American retailer Focus in its venture into the Canadian market. Target set aggressive goals connected with piece of the pie and income age however confronted difficulties connected with production network issues, stock administration, and an absence of comprehension of Canadian customer inclinations. The organization's inability to adjust its goals to the intricacies of the Canadian market added to its retreat from the country.

Moreover, the instance of the web-based entertainment stage Twitter's difficulties in growing its client base in specific global business sectors features the significance of social awareness in genuine setting. Twitter put forth objectives connected with client securing yet confronted challenges in areas where social standards and correspondence inclinations contrasted altogether. This case highlights the requirement for organizations to think about social subtleties and adjust their goals to line up with different market settings.

4.3 Strategies for product adaptation and customization

Procedures for item variation and customization are essential parts of a fruitful worldwide business technique. As organizations venture into different worldwide business sectors, they experience interesting purchaser inclinations, social subtleties, and administrative necessities. Adjusting and tweaking items to meet the particular requirements of each market is fundamental for acquiring acknowledgment, building brand faithfulness, and making supported progress. In this exhaustive investigation, we will dig into the vital techniques and contemplations organizations utilize to adjust and redo their items for worldwide business sectors actually.

Statistical surveying and Purchaser Bits of knowledge:

The underpinning of fruitful item variation and customization lies in extensive statistical surveying and grasping buyer bits of knowledge. Prior to entering another market, organizations should lead careful exploration to get a handle on the neighborhood inclinations, ways of behaving, and assumptions for purchasers. This includes examining social, monetary, and social factors that impact buying choices. By acquiring a profound comprehension of the interest group, organizations can tailor their items to line up with neighborhood tastes and inclinations.

Limitation of Highlights and Plan:

Adjusting item elements and plan to suit nearby inclinations is a key system for fruitful worldwide item customization. This might include changing item details, feel, or functionalities to all the more likely line up with the social and commonsense parts of the objective market.

For instance, in the buyer gadgets industry, organizations frequently change item sizes, varieties, and UIs to take special care of provincial inclinations. Confining elements upgrades the apparent worth of the item and builds its importance in the new market.

Bundling Variation:

Bundling fills in as an essential component of item show and can fundamentally influence purchaser discernment. Adjusting bundling to reflect neighborhood social standards, language inclinations, and plan feel is an essential methodology. Bundling shouldn't just consent to administrative necessities yet in addition resound with the interest group. Marks frequently influence variety plans, symbolism, and informing that are socially significant and interesting to the neighborhood customer, adding to a positive initial feeling.

Evaluating Procedures:

Successful estimating procedures are key parts of item variation and customization. Estimating ought to consider neighborhood financial circumstances, purchaser buying power, and serious scenes. Organizations might take on different evaluating techniques, for example, infiltration valuing to acquire portion of the overall industry or premium estimating for items situated as extravagance things. Dynamic evaluating models that record for territorial varieties and money changes add to intensity and client acknowledgment.

Consistence with Administrative Norms:

Sticking to neighborhood administrative norms and consistence necessities is non-debatable for fruitful item transformation. Each market has its own arrangement of guidelines administering item security, naming, and accreditation. Organizations should completely explore and comprehend these guidelines to guarantee that their items fulfill the fundamental guidelines. Inability to consent to administrative necessities can prompt legitimate issues, harm brand notoriety, and obstruct market passage.

Customization through Measured Plan:

Executing a measured plan approach permits organizations to make items with parts that can be effectively tweaked in light of market-explicit requirements. This technique upgrades adaptability and effectiveness in answering assorted shopper requests. By offering secluded items, organizations can collect arrangements that take special care of the inclinations of various business sectors without the requirement for broad upgrade or creation updates.

Key Coalitions and Associations:

Framing vital collusions and associations with nearby organizations can work with powerful item transformation. Teaming up with wholesalers, retailers, or producers in the objective market gives important bits of knowledge into buyer inclinations and market elements. Associations can likewise add to the improvement of confined items through joint endeavors or permitting arrangements. Utilizing the mastery of neighborhood accomplices assists organizations with exploring social subtleties and gain a more profound comprehension of the market.

Innovation driven Customization:

Progressions in innovation, especially in assembling and data frameworks, empower organizations to carry out innovation driven customization. Mass customization, controlled by computerized innovations, permits organizations to create customized items for a bigger scope effectively. For instance, adjustable elements in clothing, like size, variety, and plan choices, can be consistently coordinated into computerized stages, furnishing customers with a customized shopping experience.

Advanced Showcasing and Web based business Stages:

Advanced showcasing and web based business stages offer integral assets for fitting item contributions to explicit market sections. Organizations can utilize online examination and purchaser information to figure out the inclinations and ways of behaving of their main interest group. This data can advise the customization regarding promoting messages, item suggestions, and, surprisingly, the advancement of area explicit item variations. Internet business stages give an immediate channel to organizations to worldwide proposition tweaked items to customers.

Confined Promoting Efforts:

Fitting showcasing efforts to neighborhood societies and inclinations is fundamental for fruitful item variation. Language, symbolism, and informing ought to resound with the qualities and desires of the main interest group. Showcasing materials, including ads, limited time content, and online entertainment crusades, ought to be socially delicate and significant. Confined showcasing improves brand association, cultivates purchaser trust, and adds to the general progress of the item in the new market.

Input Systems and Persistent Improvement:

Carrying out criticism systems and channels for client input is essential for progressing item variation and customization. Organizations ought to empower client input, audits, and studies to assemble bits of knowledge into item execution and fulfillment. Nonstop observing of client opinions permits organizations to distinguish regions for development and answer quickly to changing business sector elements. This iterative interaction guarantees that items stay lined up with buyer assumptions over the long haul.

Worldwide Item Stages:

Laying out worldwide item stages includes making a center item with normalized parts that can be effectively adjusted for various business sectors. This approach smoothes out creation processes while taking into consideration local customization. The center parts stay predictable, guaranteeing brand attachment and cost-productivity, while confined components take care of explicit market inclinations. Worldwide item stages find some kind of harmony among normalization and customization, offering a versatile answer for global business sectors.

Social Awareness and Social Qualities:

Understanding the social and social upsides of the objective market is vital in item transformation. Social awareness goes past feel and reaches out to item functionalities, informing, and even brand situating. Organizations need to adjust their items to the social qualities and standards of the neighborhood populace. This incorporates contemplations like strict convictions, social practices, and moral contemplations. Adjusting items in accordance with social responsive qualities upgrades acknowledgment and cultivates positive brand discernment.

Contextual analyses Representing Fruitful Item Variation and Customization:

Inspecting contextual analyses of organizations that have effectively carried out item variation and customization procedures gives important experiences into successful methodologies. One such case is the worldwide development of the refreshment organization Coca-Cola. Coca-Cola has proficiently adjusted its items to different social inclinations while keeping a predictable brand personality. In various business sectors, Coca-Cola offers area explicit flavors, bundling sizes, and showcasing efforts that reverberate with neighborhood buyers. This approach has added to Coca-Cola's persevering through worldwide allure.

One more prominent case is the extension of the cheap food chain KFC (Kentucky Seared Chicken) into the Chinese market. KFC effectively limited its menu to take care of Chinese preferences and inclinations. Understanding the meaning of family eating in Chinese culture, KFC presented family-sized feasts and integrated nearby flavors into its contributions. The organization's accentuation on adjusting to nearby dietary patterns, for example, giving rice-based choices, added to its broad ubiquity in China.

Difficulties and Illustrations Gained from Fruitless Item Variation:

Understanding the difficulties looked by organizations with fruitless item variation is significant for inferring important illustrations. One such case is the presentation of the Portage Edsel during the 1950s. The Edsel confronted difficulties in the U.S. market because of a crisscross between its plan and shopper inclinations. In spite of broad statistical surveying, Portage misconceived the allure of specific plan highlights, bringing about an item that didn't line up with the preferences and assumptions for American shoppers. The Edsel fills in as a useful example about the significance of precisely measuring customer inclinations and assumptions during item improvement.

Furthermore, the experience of the cheap food chain McDonald's in India features the intricacies of item transformation. While McDonald's has effectively adjusted its menu in numerous worldwide business sectors, it confronted difficulties in India, where a critical part of the populace follows veggie lover eats less. The organization needed to reconfigure its menu to offer an assortment of vegan choices.

Transformation and customization assume crucial parts in the progress of organizations exploring the intricacies of a worldwide commercial center. In a period portrayed by assorted buyer inclinations, social subtleties, and administrative scenes, the capacity to fit items and administrations to meet the particular necessities of various business sectors is essential. This complete investigation dives into the multi-layered parts of transformation and customization, analyzing procedures, difficulties, and contextual analyses that enlighten the meaning of these practices in making worldwide progress.

Characterizing Variation and Customization:
Variation and customization are nuanced ideas that include fitting items, administrations, and systems to suit the unmistakable qualities of explicit business sectors or shopper fragments. While the terms are frequently utilized reciprocally, they convey various levels of change. Transformation commonly alludes to changing components of an item or system to line up with neighborhood conditions, inclinations, or guidelines. Then again, customization includes fitting items or administrations to meet the singular inclinations or necessities of explicit clients.

Market-explicit Item Transformation:
One of the principal methodologies in global business is market-explicit item variation. This includes adjusting items to take care of the remarkable inclinations and social subtleties of various business sectors. For example, purchaser gadgets organizations frequently change item highlights, plans, and functionalities to line up with neighborhood assumptions. This procedure recognizes that what works in a single market may not be guaranteed to resound in another, and fitting items in like manner is vital for acquiring acknowledgment and piece of the pie.

Confinement of Highlights and Plan:
A critical aspect of item transformation is the limitation of highlights and plan. This methodology involves changing item details, feel, or functionalities to more readily line up with the social and commonsense parts of the objective market. For instance, vehicle makers might modify vehicle highlights to oblige driving propensities common in unambiguous locales. This upgrades the significance of the item as well as mirrors a comprehension of neighborhood customer requirements and inclinations.

Bundling Transformation:
The transformation of bundling is an imperative component of item show that can essentially influence buyer discernment. Bundling transformation includes fitting the visual and educational parts of item bundling to suit neighborhood inclinations and social sensibilities. Marks frequently alter bundling plans, varieties, and symbolism to resound with the main interest group. Viable bundling transformation consents to administrative necessities as well as fills in as a useful asset for making a positive initial feeling and cultivating brand devotion.

Estimating Techniques for Neighborhood Markets:
Creating viable evaluating procedures is critical for effective item transformation. Valuing should consider neighborhood financial circumstances, shopper buying power, and cutthroat scenes. Organizations might embrace district explicit estimating models, changing costs to line up with economic situations. Dynamic valuing procedures that record for cash vacillations and neighborhood cost structures add to intensity and client acknowledgment. By fitting valuing procedures to neighborhood settings, organizations can streamline income age while staying cutthroat.

Social Awareness and Moral Contemplations:

EXPORT STRATEGIES

A foundation of effective variation is social responsiveness. Grasping the social qualities, standards, and moral contemplations of an objective market is vital. Items and showcasing methodologies should line up with nearby traditions to stay away from social stumbles. Moral contemplations, like adjusting items to feasible practices or staying away from socially unfeeling informing, assume a pivotal part in building trust and generosity. Inability to represent social subtleties can prompt reputational harm and block market acknowledgment.

Administrative Consistence:

Adherence to neighborhood administrative guidelines is non-debatable in worldwide business. Items should conform to assorted guidelines administering security, naming, and accreditation in each market. Inability to go along can bring about lawful confusions, item reviews, and harm to mark notoriety. Fruitful variation includes careful exploration and comprehension of the administrative scene in each target market. Organizations should explore complex administrative structures to guarantee that their items satisfy the essential guidelines and necessities.

Customization through Measured Plan:

Executing a measured plan approach permits organizations to make items with parts that can be effortlessly tweaked in light of market-explicit requirements. This system upgrades adaptability and proficiency in answering assorted buyer requests. By offering particular items, organizations can collect setups that take special care of the inclinations of various business sectors without the requirement for broad upgrade or creation updates. Particular plan works with smoothed out customization while keeping up with center item consistency.

Vital Unions and Associations:

Shaping key unions and organizations with neighborhood organizations is a co-operative way to deal with item transformation. Organizations give significant bits of knowledge into buyer inclinations and market elements, directing the transformation interaction. Teaming up with merchants, retailers, or producers in the objective market permits organizations to use nearby mastery. Vital partnerships can likewise add to the advancement of limited items through joint endeavors or authorizing arrangements, working with smoother market passage.

Innovation driven Customization:

Progressions in innovation have changed the customization scene. Innovation driven customization use advanced apparatuses and fabricating cycles to offer customized items at scale. Mass customization, empowered by computerized advances, permits organizations to effectively deliver merchandise custom-made to individual inclinations. For example, adjustable elements in clothing, like size, variety, and plan choices, can be flawlessly coordinated into computerized stages, furnishing customers with a customized shopping experience.

Computerized Advertising and Internet business Stages:

Computerized promoting and online business stages are useful assets for fitting items and administrations to explicit market sections. These stages give an abundance of information and examination that organizations can use to figure out buyer inclinations. Computerized promoting efforts can be redone to target explicit socioeconomics, and internet business stages offer the adaptability to feature an assorted scope of items custom-made to various business sectors. The information driven nature of computerized channels upgrades the accuracy of customization techniques.

Restricted Showcasing Efforts:

Fitting promoting efforts to neighborhood societies and inclinations is instrumental in fruitful item variation. Language, symbolism, and informing ought to resound with the qualities and desires of the interest group. Showcasing materials, including commercials, special substance, and online entertainment crusades, ought to be socially delicate and important. Limited advertising upgrades brand association, encourages customer trust, and adds to the general progress of the item in the new market.

Input Components and Persistent Improvement:

Carrying out criticism components and channels for client input is essential for progressing item variation and customization. Organizations ought to energize client criticism, audits, and reviews to assemble bits of knowledge into item execution and fulfillment. Constant observing of client feelings permits organizations to distinguish regions for development and answer quickly to changing business sector elements. This iterative cycle guarantees that items stay lined up with buyer assumptions over the long haul.

Worldwide Item Stages:

Laying out worldwide item stages includes making a center item with normalized parts that can be effectively adjusted for various business sectors. This approach smoothes out creation processes while considering local customization. The center parts stay steady, guaranteeing brand attachment and cost-effectiveness, while confined components take care of explicit market inclinations. Worldwide item stages find some kind of harmony among normalization and customization, offering a versatile answer for global business sectors.

Social Awareness and Social Qualities:

Understanding the social and social upsides of the objective market is foremost in item transformation. Social responsiveness goes past style and stretches out to item functionalities, informing, and even brand situating. Organizations need to adjust their items to the social qualities and standards of the nearby populace. This incorporates contemplations like strict convictions, social customs, and moral contemplations. Adjusting items in accordance with social responsive qualities upgrades acknowledgment and cultivates positive brand discernment.

Contextual analyses Delineating Effective Variation and Customization:

Analyzing contextual investigations of organizations that have effectively executed variation and customization systems gives important experiences into successful methodologies. One such case is the worldwide development of the drink organization Coca-Cola. Coca-Cola has capably adjusted its items to different social inclinations while keeping a reliable brand character. In various business sectors, Coca-Cola offers area explicit flavors, bundling sizes, and advertising efforts that resound with nearby buyers. This approach has added to Coca-Cola's persevering through worldwide allure.

One more striking case is the extension of the cheap food chain KFC (Kentucky Seared Chicken) into the Chinese market. KFC effectively restricted its menu to take special care of Chinese preferences and inclinations. Understanding the meaning of family feasting in Chinese culture, KFC presented family-sized dinners and integrated neighborhood flavors into its contributions. The organization's accentuation on adjusting to neighborhood dietary patterns, for example, giving rice-based choices, added to its far and wide ubiquity in China.

Difficulties and Illustrations Gained from Fruitless Transformation:
Understanding the difficulties looked by organizations with ineffective variation is urgent for inferring important illustrations. One such case is the presentation of the Portage Edsel during the 1950s. The Edsel confronted difficulties in the U.S. market because of a befuddle between its plan and purchaser inclinations. Regardless of broad statistical surveying, Portage misconstrued the allure of specific plan highlights, bringing about an item that didn't line up with the preferences and assumptions for American shoppers. The Edsel fills in as a wake up call about the significance of precisely measuring customer inclinations and assumptions during item improvement.

Moreover, the experience of the cheap food chain McDonald's in India features the intricacies of item variation. While McDonald's has effectively adjusted its menu in numerous worldwide business sectors, it confronted difficulties in India, where a huge piece of the populace follows vegan counts calories. The organization needed to reconfigure its menu to offer an assortment of veggie lover choices, including items customized to nearby preferences. This case highlights the significance of thinking about dietary inclinations and social awarenesses in item transformation.

Chapter 5

Legal and Regulatory Considerations

Lawful and administrative contemplations assume a urgent part in forming the scene of different ventures, impacting how organizations work and communicate with their partners. These contemplations incorporate a great many regulations, guidelines, and consistence prerequisites that organizations should explore to guarantee moral practices, safeguard partners' inclinations, and keep a fair and cutthroat commercial center.

At the center of legitimate contemplations for organizations is the need to agree with nearby, public, and global regulations. These regulations cover different regions like agreement regulation, licensed innovation, business, ecological guidelines, customer insurance, and that's just the beginning. Understanding and sticking to these legitimate structures is fundamental for organizations to work inside the limits set by the general set of laws and stay away from legitimate entanglements.

One basic part of legitimate consistence is contract regulation, which administers the arrangements between parties. Contracts are the groundwork of business connections, framing the privileges, commitments, and obligations of each party included. Inability to follow legally binding commitments can prompt legitimate questions, monetary misfortunes, and harm to a business' standing. In this manner, organizations should cautiously draft, survey, and uphold agreements to guarantee lawful lucidity and stay away from possible legitimate traps.

Protected innovation (IP) regulations are one more vital part of lawful contemplations. These regulations safeguard immaterial resources like licenses, brand names, copyrights, and proprietary innovations. Protecting licensed innovation is indispensable for encouraging advancement and innovativeness inside enterprises. Infringement of IP privileges can bring about lawful activity, monetary punishments, and reputational harm. Organizations need to carry out strong techniques to safeguard their protected innovation and regard the privileges of others to keep a fair and serious commercial center.

EXPORT STRATEGIES

Business regulations are necessary to guaranteeing fair and moral treatment of representatives. These regulations oversee perspectives like wages, working hours, work environment wellbeing, separation, and end methodology.

Consistence with business regulations encourages a positive workplace as well as assists organizations with staying away from lawful liabilities and keep a roused and useful labor force. Organizations working across borders should likewise consider worldwide business regulations to guarantee worldwide consistence.

Natural guidelines have acquired unmistakable quality as social orders become more aware of the effect of business exercises on the climate. Consistence with natural regulations is fundamental for manageable strategic approaches, lessening environmental impressions, and limiting unfriendly consequences for biological systems. Resistance can prompt lawful outcomes, public investigation, and harm to an organization's corporate picture. Thusly, organizations should incorporate natural contemplations into their activities and embrace harmless to the ecosystem rehearses.

Purchaser insurance regulations are intended to shield the privileges and interests of shoppers. These regulations direct fair strategic approaches, item wellbeing guidelines, and straightforward correspondence. Consistence with purchaser insurance regulations is basic for building entrust with clients and keeping away from legitimate activities connected with misleading communication, item deserts, or unreasonable strategic policies. Also, organizations should remain informed about arising issues in buyer security to as needs be adjust their practices.

In the always developing advanced scene, information security and protection regulations have become progressively huge. The expansion of computerized innovations and the immense measures of information produced expect organizations to mindfully deal with individual and delicate data. Legitimate structures like the Overall Information Security Guideline (GDPR) in the European Association set tough norms for information assurance and protection. Organizations should carry out powerful information insurance arrangements, guarantee secure treatment of information, and get express agree from people to keep away from legitimate repercussions.

Antitrust and rivalry regulations expect to cultivate fair contest and forestall monopolistic practices that could hurt purchasers or different organizations. These regulations forbid exercises, for example, cost fixing, market allotment, and monopolistic consolidations. Adherence to antitrust guidelines advances solid market rivalry, shields customers from unjustifiable strategic policies, and adds to a level battleground for organizations.

In the domain of monetary guidelines, organizations should explore a perplexing snare of rules overseeing monetary exchanges, revealing, and straightforwardness. Monetary guidelines intend to guarantee the solidness of monetary business sectors, forestall extortion, and safeguard financial backers.

Rebelliousness with monetary guidelines can prompt serious results, including legitimate punishments, monetary misfortunes, and reputational harm. Along these lines, organizations should have strong monetary administration and announcing systems set up to meet administrative necessities.

Worldwide organizations face the extra test of exploring global exchange regulations and arrangements. Grasping the complexities of economic alliance, duties, and product import guidelines is pivotal for organizations taken part in cross-line exercises. Global exchange regulations not just direct how labor and products can get across borders yet in addition impact political and financial connections between nations. Organizations should remain informed about changes in worldwide exchange regulations to adjust their systems and keep up with consistence.

The rise of computerized monetary standards and blockchain innovation has acquainted another aspect with lawful and administrative contemplations. Legislatures and administrative bodies are wrestling with how to manage cryptographic forms of money, starting coin contributions (ICOs), and blockchain-based exchanges. The advancing idea of this innovation expects organizations to keep up to date with administrative turns of events and adjust their practices to follow arising lawful structures.

Online protection guidelines have acquired unmistakable quality as the recurrence and refinement of digital dangers keep on rising. Legislatures and administrative bodies are ordering regulations to safeguard delicate information, forestall cyberattacks, and consider organizations responsible for information breaks. Consistence with online protection guidelines is critical for keeping up with the trust of clients and defending classified data. Organizations should put resources into vigorous network protection measures, lead customary reviews, and remain informed about the advancing danger scene.

The legitimate scene isn't static; it develops in light of cultural changes, mechanical progressions, and arising worldwide difficulties. Organizations should take on a proactive way to deal with lawful contemplations, remaining informed about official changes, court choices, and administrative updates. This requires laying out successful instruments for legitimate examination, drawing in with lawful experts, and coordinating legitimate consistence into the general business technique.

Notwithstanding consistence, organizations should likewise think about moral contemplations in their tasks. Moral practices go past simple lawful necessities and include directing business in a way that lines up with moral standards and cultural qualities. While regulations give a structure to satisfactory way of behaving, moral contemplations guide organizations in settling on choices that contribute emphatically to society, the climate, and the prosperity of partners.

Corporate administration, enveloping the arrangement of rules, practices, and cycles by which an organization is coordinated and controlled, is fundamental to tending to lawful and moral contemplations. Successful corporate administration guarantees straightforwardness, responsibility, and reasonableness in navigation. It includes the conveyance of limitations among various partners, including investors, the executives, and the top managerial staff. Sticking to sound corporate administration standards is fundamental for building trust, drawing in venture, and supporting long haul business achievement.

Lawful and administrative consistence isn't just a case ticking exercise; it is an essential basic for organizations looking for life span and versatility. Resistance can bring about serious results, including legitimate activities, monetary punishments, harmed notorieties, and loss of portion of the overall industry. Subsequently, organizations should focus on legitimate contemplations as a fundamental piece of their gamble the board and key arranging processes.

All in all, legitimate and administrative contemplations are fundamental to the working of organizations in the present perplexing and interconnected world. Exploring the perplexing snare of regulations and guidelines requires a thorough comprehension of the lawful scene, a promise to moral practices, and proactive commitment with legitimate experts. By incorporating lawful contemplations into their tasks, organizations can encourage a culture of consistence, moderate dangers, and add to a fair and feasible business climate.

5.1 Overview of international trade laws and regulations

Worldwide exchange regulations and guidelines structure the system that administers the trading of labor and products across borders. In a globalized world, where organizations progressively participate in cross-line exchanges, understanding and complying to these regulations are pivotal for encouraging fair exchange works on, guaranteeing consistence, and keeping away from legitimate complexities. This outline investigates the vital parts of worldwide exchange regulations, addressing economic deals, levies, import and product guidelines, and the job of global associations in forming the worldwide exchange scene.

At the core of worldwide exchange regulation are economic alliance, which are settlements between nations that characterize the agreements under which they participate in business. These arrangements can take different structures, going from respective arrangements between two countries to multilateral arrangements including various nations. Respective arrangements lay out exchange relations between two countries, illustrating the principles for imports, sends out, and other exchange related matters. Multilateral arrangements, then again, include various nations and frequently plan to make a more comprehensive and normalized way to deal with worldwide exchange.

One of the most notable multilateral economic alliance is the World Exchange Association (WTO). Laid out in 1995, the WTO fills in as a worldwide gathering for arranging economic deals, settling exchange debates, and checking the execution of exchange strategies.

The WTO's essential goal is to advance open and fair exchange rehearses by giving a stage to part nations to arrange and settle on exchange related matters. The association works on the standards of non-separation, straightforwardness, and the advancement of fair rivalry.

Provincial economic accords are one more basic element of worldwide exchange regulations. These arrangements include gatherings of nations inside a particular geological district and are intended to work with exchange and monetary participation among part states. Models incorporate the North American International alliance (NAFTA), which developed into the US Mexico-Canada Understanding (USMCA), and the European Association (EU), which works as a solitary market with a typical exchange strategy among its part states.

Taxes assume a huge part in global exchange, impacting the expense of products and influencing exchange streams between nations. A levy is an expense forced by an administration on imported or sent out merchandise. Duties can be explicit, in view of the amount of merchandise, or promotion valorem, determined as a level of the item's worth. Taxes fill different needs, for example, creating income for the public authority, shielding homegrown businesses from unfamiliar contest, and empowering the utilization of locally delivered products.

Exchange progression, the decrease or end of exchange hindrances, is a predominant pattern in worldwide economic deals. Nations haggle to bring down levies, work on customs systems, and decrease different boundaries to advance free and open exchange. The objective is to make a level battleground, invigorate monetary development, and give purchasers a more extensive scope of decisions at cutthroat costs.

Import and commodity guidelines are basic parts of worldwide exchange regulations, administering the development of merchandise across borders. These guidelines incorporate a great many necessities, including customs documentation, permitting, naming, and quality principles. Complying with these guidelines is fundamental for organizations to guarantee smooth cross-line exchanges and stay away from deferrals or punishments.

Customs obligations are charges imposed on products as they cross worldwide boundaries. These obligations add to government income and can shift generally contingent upon the sort of merchandise and the nations in question. Customs specialists assume a significant part in upholding import and product guidelines, reviewing merchandise, and guaranteeing consistence with pertinent regulations. Organizations participated in global exchange should explore the mind boggling scene of customs strategies to work with the effective development of products.

Rules of beginning are one more key part of worldwide exchange guidelines. These principles decide the public wellspring of an item and are pivotal for applying duties and exchange inclinations.

Understanding and conforming to rules of beginning is fundamental for organizations to profit from special economic accords, like diminished taxes or obligation free admittance to specific business sectors. Resistance can bring about greater expenses and a deficiency of upper hand.

Exchange cures are measures that state run administrations can take to address unreasonable exchange rehearses and safeguard homegrown enterprises. These cures

EXPORT STRATEGIES

incorporate enemy of unloading obligations, balancing obligations, and protections. Hostile to unloading obligations are forced on imported products that are sold at costs lower than their honest evaluation, balancing obligations target sponsored imports that hurt homegrown businesses, and shields are transitory measures to safeguard homegrown ventures confronting a flood in imports.

Question goal systems are vital to the adequacy of worldwide exchange regulations. The WTO gives a stage to part nations to determine exchange questions through an organized interaction. Debates might emerge when a nation accepts that another part's exchange strategies or practices disregard WTO arrangements. The debate goal process includes interview, intercession, and, if fundamental, settlement by a board of specialists. Consistence with debate goal results is significant for keeping up with the validity and adequacy of the worldwide exchange framework.

Licensed innovation privileges (IPR) are a basic thought in global exchange, especially in accordance with the security of licenses, brand names, copyrights, and proprietary advantages. Peaceful accords, for example, the Settlement on Exchange Related Parts of Licensed innovation Freedoms (Excursions) set norms for the insurance and requirement of licensed innovation on a worldwide scale. Organizations participated in global exchange should explore IPR contemplations to safeguard their developments and manifestations and keep away from legitimate questions.

Endorses and bans are instruments utilized by states to impact the way of behaving of different nations. Sanctions include limitations on exchange, monetary exchanges, or other financial exercises, while bans deny all exchange with a specific country. These actions are frequently utilized for political or security reasons and can have critical ramifications for organizations took part in global exchange. Understanding and agreeing with sanctions and bans are fundamental to keep away from legitimate repercussions and reputational harm.

As of late, natural manageability has turned into an undeniably significant thought in worldwide exchange. Economic accords might incorporate arrangements connected with natural guidelines, preservation measures, and reasonable practices. Organizations are feeling the squeeze to show natural obligation in their stockpile chains and tasks. Sticking to natural norms guarantees consistence with economic alliance as well as adds to the worldwide work to address environmental change and advance manageable turn of events.

Common liberties contemplations are additionally acquiring conspicuousness in global exchange conversations. Economic deals might incorporate arrangements connected with work privileges, fair wages, and working circumstances. Organizations are supposed to stick to moral work practices and regard basic liberties all through their stock chains. Inability to do so can prompt reputational harm and lawful results, as buyers and partners progressively request socially mindful strategic policies.

The digitalization of business has presented new difficulties and open doors in worldwide exchange. Online business, advanced administrations, and information streams are vital to present day exchange, and states are wrestling with how to really direct these angles. Guaranteeing the free progression of information while tending to protection and security concerns is a perplexing undertaking. Global exchange regulations are advancing to address the remarkable difficulties presented by the computerized economy, expecting organizations to keep up to date with administrative turns of events.

All in all, worldwide exchange regulations and guidelines structure a complicated and dynamic system that oversees the worldwide trade of labor and products. Organizations participated in worldwide exchange should explore a diverse scene of economic deals, taxes, import and product guidelines, and consistence prerequisites. Remaining informed about changes in worldwide exchange regulations, taking part in proactive consistence endeavors, and utilizing debate goal components are fundamental for organizations to flourish in the worldwide commercial center. As the world turns out to be more interconnected, the job of worldwide exchange regulations will keep on advancing, forming the fate of worldwide trade.

5.2 Compliance requirements for exporting goods and services

Sending out labor and products across borders is an intricate cycle that includes adherence to different consistence necessities. These prerequisites are set up to guarantee the smooth progression of worldwide exchange, safeguard public interests, and keep a level battleground for organizations. Exploring the complexities of product consistence is fundamental for organizations hoping to grow their market reach and take part in cross-line exchanges. This exhaustive outline dives into the key consistence contemplations for sending out labor and products, covering regions, for example, trade controls, documentation, sanctions, and the job of administrative bodies.

Trade controls are administrative measures forced by states to oversee and screen the product of explicit merchandise and advances. The essential objective is to forestall the unapproved move of things that could present dangers to public safety, public wellbeing, or international strategy interests. These controls change from one country to another and are in many cases in view of peaceful accords and settlements. Organizations associated with trading labor and products should know about send out control guidelines to guarantee consistence with the laws of both the sending out and bringing in nations.

One crucial part of commodity controls is the control of double use things — products, programming, or innovation that have both regular citizen and military applications. States control the commodity of double use things to forestall their utilization in exercises that could subvert security or add to the advancement of weapons of mass obliteration. Organizations should order their items precisely to decide if they fall under the class of double use things and are likely to send out controls.

Send out permitting is a vital part of commodity controls, expecting organizations to get government approval prior to trading specific labor and products. Permitting assists states with evaluating the potential dangers related with explicit products and guarantees that they line up with public interests and peaceful accords. The permitting system includes submitting point by point data about the labor and products, end-clients, and planned use, permitting specialists to settle on informed conclusions about whether to allow endorsement.

Understanding the end-use and end-client of sent out merchandise is critical for send out consistence. State run administrations are worried about the likely redirection of merchandise to unapproved parties or for unapproved purposes. Organizations should lead an expected level of effort to confirm the authenticity of their clients and the planned utilization of the sent out things. This might include screening clients against confined party records and leading gamble evaluations to distinguish any warnings that might show likely abuse.

Documentation assumes a focal part in send out consistence, giving a path of data that specialists can use to confirm the lawfulness and authenticity of worldwide exchange exchanges. Trade documentation incorporates the business receipt, pressing rundown, bill of filling, and a declaration of beginning. Notwithstanding these standard archives, certain products might require explicit commodity licenses, declarations, or grants. Exact and finish documentation is fundamental for customs freedom and consistence with trade guidelines.

Send out characterization is the most common way of relegating a particular code to an item founded on its qualities, sythesis, and expected use. These codes, frequently alluded to as Fit Framework (HS) or Timetable B numbers, assist with normalizing the characterization of products for customs purposes. The right order is basic for deciding the appropriate commodity controls, duties, and authorizing necessities. Organizations should put time and assets in guaranteeing precise item arrangement to stay away from consistence issues.

Send out consistence additionally reaches out to the thought of monetary authorizations forced by legislatures on unambiguous nations, elements, or people. Sanctions are a device used to impact the way of behaving of designated elements or to address public safety concerns. Organizations should screen all gatherings associated with a commodity exchange against officially sanctioned arrangements of endorsed substances. These rundowns, frequently kept up with by administrative bodies, incorporate people, organizations, and nations subject to exchange limitations.

Sending out to endorsed nations or elements without the suitable licenses is a serious infringement of commodity guidelines and can bring about extreme punishments. Assents might remember limitations for explicit merchandise, administrations, monetary exchanges, or speculations. Remaining informed about changes to sanctions records and routinely screening colleagues is fundamental for consistence. Obliviousness of approvals or inability to direct reasonable level of effort can prompt lawful results and reputational harm.

Send out consistence isn't just about gathering the necessities of the trading nation yet additionally includes figuring out the guidelines of the bringing in country. Import guidelines differ broadly, and organizations should know about the particular necessities and limitations forced by the objective country. This incorporates consistence with customs strategies, documentation prerequisites, and a particular item guidelines or confirmations commanded by the bringing in country.

Exchange money and installment techniques are necessary parts of product consistence. Organizations should think about the monetary parts of global exchange exchanges, including the terms of installment, letters of credit, and commodity funding. Letters of credit give a protected strategy for installment for exporters, guaranteeing that they get installment after gathering the predefined conditions. Exporters should find out more about the agreements of letters of credit to guarantee consistence and stay away from monetary dangers.

Send out funding choices, for example, send out credit protection and product working capital, can assist with relieving the monetary dangers related with worldwide exchange. Send out credit protection safeguards organizations against the gamble of non-installment by unfamiliar purchasers, while trade working capital gives financing to help the creation and product of merchandise. Using these monetary devices in consistence with guidelines assists organizations with overseeing gambles and work with worldwide exchange exchanges.

Incoterms, or Worldwide Business Terms, are normalized exchange terms that characterize the obligations and liabilities of purchasers and dealers in global exchange exchanges. Incoterms indicate the conveyance point, move of hazard, and the party liable for transportation and protection costs. Understanding and consolidating the fitting Incoterms in deals is fundamental for clear correspondence and consistence with exchange guidelines. The decision of Incoterms likewise influences the general expense design of global exchange exchanges.

Exchange hindrances, including portions, bans, and exchange limitations, can altogether affect send out consistence. Standards limit the amount of specific products that can be sent out or imported inside a predefined period. Bans force a total restriction on exchange with explicit nations or substances. Exchange limitations might incorporate permitting prerequisites, item norms, or marking necessities. Organizations should remain informed about exchange hindrances forced by both trading and bringing in nations to guarantee consistence and explore possible difficulties.

Customs consistence is a basic thought in the product cycle. Customs specialists assume a focal part in confirming the precision of product documentation, surveying obligations and charges, and guaranteeing that merchandise follow relevant guidelines. Rebelliousness with customs techniques can prompt postponements, fines, and the capture of products. Organizations should carry out strong traditions consistence works on, including precise item order, appropriate valuation, and adherence to customs documentation necessities.

Notwithstanding public guidelines, organizations took part in worldwide exchange should think about the effect of local economic alliance. Territorial arrangements, like international alliances (FTAs) and customs associations, make special exchange conditions among part nations. Exploiting these arrangements requires understanding the principles of beginning, which decide if an item fits the bill for special treatment in view of its starting point. Consistence with local economic deals can prompt expense reserve funds, expanded market access, and upper hands for exporters.

Innovation assumes an essential part in improving product consistence endeavors. Send out administration programming and robotization devices assist organizations with smoothing out processes, oversee documentation, and guarantee exactness in item order. These devices can likewise help with screening colleagues against confined party records and remaining refreshed on changes to trade controls and endorses. Putting resources into innovation arrangements adds to effectiveness and precision in send out consistence.

Production network security is a developing worry with regards to trade consistence. State run administrations are progressively centered around getting worldwide stockpile chains to forestall the unapproved development of products and improve by and large security. Organizations should execute store network safety efforts, like the utilization of secure bundling, global positioning frameworks, and hazard evaluations, to consent to security guidelines and shield their stockpile chains from possible dangers.

Preparing and training are necessary parts of a fruitful product consistence program. Representatives associated with worldwide exchange should be all around informed about trade guidelines, consistence prerequisites, and the potential dangers related with resistance. Preparing projects ought to cover regions, for example, send out controls, sanctions, documentation prerequisites, and a reasonable level of effort rehearses. Putting resources into continuous training guarantees that the labor force stays mindful of administrative changes and best practices in send out compliance.

5.3 Mitigating legal risks in foreign markets

Venturing into unfamiliar business sectors presents rewarding open doors for organizations looking for development and expansion. Nonetheless, it likewise presents a horde of legitimate dangers that can have huge outcomes while possibly not enough tended to. Relieving legitimate dangers in unfamiliar business sectors requires an extensive methodology that envelops lawful reasonable level of effort, consistence with nearby regulations, successful agreement the executives, and question goal systems.

This outline digs into key contemplations and techniques for organizations expecting to explore and limit lawful dangers in their worldwide undertakings.

Lawful Reasonable level of effort:

Prior to entering an unfamiliar market, it is foremost to lead intensive legitimate reasonable level of effort. This cycle includes a top to bottom assessment of the lawful scene in the objective nation, distinguishing possible dangers, and grasping the administrative climate. Key parts of lawful reasonable level of effort include:

1. **Administrative Consistence:** Understanding and consenting to nearby regulations and guidelines is crucial. This incorporates work regulations, charge guidelines, ecological prerequisites, and industry-explicit guidelines. Rebelliousness can prompt legitimate difficulties, fines, and reputational harm.
2. **Political and Financial Steadiness:** Surveying the political and monetary solidness of the objective nation is urgent. Political flimsiness and monetary vulnerabilities can affect business activities and open organizations to legitimate dangers. Checking government approaches and expected changes in administration is fundamental.
3. **Licensed innovation Privileges:** Safeguarding protected innovation (IP) is crucial for organizations entering unfamiliar business sectors. This includes surveying the strength of IP regulations in the objective nation, getting licenses and brand names, and executing procedures to forestall encroachment.
4. **Legally binding Arrangements:** Auditing and understanding nearby agreement regulations is fundamental for drafting and arranging arrangements. This incorporates circulation arrangements, joint endeavors, and authorizing plans. Clearness in authoritative terms can assist with moderating legitimate questions.
5. **Information Security and Security:** With the rising spotlight on information insurance, organizations should guarantee consistence with nearby information protection regulations. Understanding how information is gathered, put away, and handled in the objective nation is urgent to stay away from lawful repercussions.

Consistence with Nearby Regulations:

Nearby lawful consistence is a foundation of hazard moderation in unfamiliar business sectors. Complying with nearby regulations and guidelines guarantees lawful remaining as well as adds to a positive standing in the host country. Key parts of consistence include:

1. **Laying out Legitimate Presence:** Deciding the fitting lawful design for tasks in an unfamiliar market is fundamental. This might include setting up a neighborhood auxiliary, framing a joint endeavor, or going into organizations. Each construction has lawful ramifications that should be thought of.
2. **Business Regulations:** Following neighborhood business regulations is basic to keeping an agreeable workplace and keeping away from lawful questions. This incorporates adherence to employing works on, working hours, leave strategies, and end methodology.
3. **Charge Consistence:** Understanding and it is basic to comply to neighborhood charge guidelines. This includes appropriate duty arranging, guaranteeing exact monetary detailing, and remaining informed about changes in charge regulations that might affect the business.

4. **Against Debasement and Pay off Regulations:** Numerous nations have rigid enemy of defilement and pay off regulations. Organizations should execute powerful enemy of defilement approaches, direct preparation for representatives, and lay out instruments to forestall and distinguish degenerate practices.
5. **Natural Guidelines:** Consistence with ecological regulations is vital for organizations, particularly those in enterprises with likely ecological effects. This might include getting licenses, overseeing waste mindfully, and taking on manageable practices.

Viable Agreement The board:

Contracts are the underpinning of business connections, and successful agreement the board is fundamental for relieving lawful dangers. Organizations ought to take on prescribed procedures in agreement drafting, exchange, and authorization. Key contemplations include:

1. **Clear and Complete Agreements:** Agreements ought to be clear, far reaching, and custom fitted to the lawful structure of the host country. Ambiguities and ambiguous language can prompt errors and legitimate debates.
2. **Restriction of Agreements:** Adjusting agreements to nearby legitimate subtleties is significant. Working with legitimate experts acquainted with the neighborhood general set of laws can assist with guaranteeing that agreements line up with nearby regulations and customs.
3. **Question Goal Systems:** Remembering successful debate goal instruments for contracts is fundamental. This might include indicating intervention strategies, picking a nonpartisan locale, or integrating elective question goal techniques.
4. **Administrative Changes and Updates:** Agreements ought to incorporate arrangements that address the effect of administrative changes. Organizations need systems to overhaul contracts because of adjustments in neighborhood regulations that might influence the agreements.
5. **Consistence Checking:** Carrying out frameworks to screen and guarantee continuous consistence with legally binding commitments is indispensable. Ordinary audits and evaluations can assist with recognizing possible issues before they grow into legitimate questions.

Debate Goal Procedures:

In spite of preventive measures, lawful debates might in any case emerge. Executing successful question goal procedures is fundamental for limiting the effect of debates on business tasks. Key procedures include:

1. **Elective Debate Goal (ADR):** ADR strategies, like discretion and intercession, offer options in contrast to conventional suit. These cycles can be quicker, more practical, and give organizations more command over the goal of debates.
2. **Decision of Regulation and Locale:** In worldwide agreements, determining the decision of regulation and ward is pivotal. Organizations ought to painstakingly consider the general set of laws under which questions will be settled and select a locale that is nonpartisan and perceived for its legitimate mastery.
3. **Cross-Line Suit Contemplations:** In the event that prosecution ends up being undeniable, organizations should be ready for cross-line judicial procedures. This includes understanding the intricacies of global case, potential requirement challenges, and drawing in lawful guidance with skill in cross-line questions.
4. **Protection Inclusion:** Assessing protection choices, for example, exchange credit protection or lawful cost protection, can give an extra layer of insurance. These strategies can assist with moderating monetary dangers related with lawful questions.
5. **Relationship The executives:** Even amidst a debate, keeping up with open lines of correspondence with the other party can be valuable. Investigating friendly goals and settlement choices can safeguard connections and limit the effect on continuous business tasks.

Emergency The executives and Correspondence:

Notwithstanding legitimate difficulties, successful emergency the executives and correspondence are significant. Organizations ought to foster emergency reaction designs that include:

1. **Legitimate Emergency Group:** Laying out a lawful emergency supervisory crew involving legitimate specialists, correspondence experts, and important partners guarantees a planned reaction to lawful difficulties.
2. **Correspondence Conventions:** Obviously characterized correspondence conventions assist with overseeing outer and inside informing during a legitimate emergency. Keeping up with straightforwardness while safeguarding delicate data is critical to protecting trust.
3. **Government and Advertising:** Drawing in with government specialists and overseeing advertising can be basic during lawful difficulties. Organizations ought to be ready to address requests from administrative bodies, media, and the general population.
4. **Consistence Reviews and Audits:**

Standard consistence reviews and audits are fundamental for progressing risk relief. Organizations ought to:

1. **Direct Intermittent Reviews:** Consistently surveying and inspecting consistence with neighborhood regulations, guidelines, and inside arrangements distinguishes areas of expected risk and rebelliousness.
2. **Update Approaches:** As regulations and guidelines advance, organizations should refresh their inner strategies likewise. This remembers changes for business regulations, information insurance guidelines, and other applicable legitimate structures.
3. **Representative Preparation:** Giving continuous preparation to workers on legitimate consistence is fundamental. This guarantees that the labor force stays mindful of legitimate prerequisites and follows best practices.
4. **Outsider Expected level of effort:** If working with outsiders, leading reasonable level of investment on accomplices, providers, and merchants is significant. Guaranteeing that outsiders consent to lawful principles can alleviate gambles related with their activities.

Carrying on with work in unfamiliar business sectors presents various open doors for development and extension, however it additionally accompanies its reasonable part of dangers and difficulties. As organizations adventure past their homegrown boundaries, they open themselves to various variables that can affect their prosperity. Understanding and alleviating these dangers is significant for any association meaning to flourish in the worldwide commercial center.

One of the essential dangers in unfamiliar business sectors is political shakiness. Political changes, like government unsteadiness, changes in authority, or political distress, can fundamentally influence the business climate. At times, unexpected approach changes or government intercessions can upset activities and effect productivity. Organizations need to intently screen the political scene of the nations they work in and be ready to adjust to changes.

Another huge gamble is monetary vulnerability. Monetary circumstances can fluctuate broadly starting with one country then onto the next, and factors, for example, expansion rates, trade rates, and financial slumps can straightforwardly affect business activities. Cash vacillations, for example, can influence the expense of imports and products, possibly prompting monetary misfortunes. Financial instability can likewise affect shopper buying power, impacting interest for items and administrations.

Social contrasts represent an extraordinary arrangement of difficulties for organizations working in unfamiliar business sectors. Errors or misinterpretations of social standards can prompt correspondence breakdowns and frustrate successful business connections.

Organizations need to put resources into social knowledge and adjust their showcasing techniques to resound with neighborhood societies. Inability to do so may bring about items or administrations that come up short with regards to social significance.

Legitimate and administrative difficulties are additionally predominant in unfamiliar business sectors. Every nation has its own arrangement of regulations, guidelines, and consistence necessities, and exploring this complicated scene can dismay. Inability to conform to nearby regulations can prompt legitimate difficulties, fines, and harm to the organization's standing. It is fundamental for organizations to lead exhaustive legitimate exploration and work intimately with nearby lawful specialists to guarantee consistence with every significant guideline.

Market contest is escalated in unfamiliar business sectors, as organizations frequently face neighborhood contenders as well as other global players. Understanding the cutthroat scene and creating compelling procedures to separate items or administrations is vital for progress. At times, nearby contenders might have a superior comprehension of the market and laid out connections, making it trying for new participants to acquire a traction.

Foundation difficulties can block business tasks in unfamiliar business sectors. Issues, for example, lacking transportation, inconsistent energy sources, or deficient media communications framework can upset supply chains and coordinated factors. Organizations should cautiously evaluate the foundation of possible business sectors and be ready to put resources into upgrades if fundamental. Inability to address these difficulties can prompt inflated costs and functional shortcomings.

Cash and monetary dangers are intrinsic while working in unfamiliar business sectors. Changes in return rates can affect the expense of merchandise, administrations, and bringing home of benefits. Organizations need to execute successful gamble the board procedures, like supporting, to relieve the effect of money unpredictability on their monetary execution. Inability to oversee money dangers can bring about huge monetary misfortunes.

Licensed innovation (IP) security is a basic worry in unfamiliar business sectors. Various nations have fluctuating degrees of IP insurance, and some might have careless implementation of copyright, brand name, and patent regulations. This seriously jeopardizes organizations of having their advancements and brand resources split the difference. Organizations must proactively shield their protected innovation through lawful means and go to lengths to forestall encroachment.

Production network disturbances can happen because of different variables, including catastrophic events, international occasions, and worldwide pandemics. The Coronavirus pandemic, for instance, featured the weakness of worldwide stockpile chains. Organizations need to evaluate the versatility of their stock chains and carry out alternate courses of action to alleviate the effect of unexpected occasions. Differentiating providers and having elective strategies courses can assist with decreasing the gamble of production network disturbances.

Defilement and pay off are normal difficulties in a few unfamiliar business sectors. In specific areas, untrustworthy strategic approaches might be imbued in the nearby business culture, making it hard for organizations to work morally while staying serious. Severe adherence to against debasement regulations and the execution of powerful consistence programs are fundamental to stay away from legitimate repercussions and harm to the organization's standing.

Social and natural variables can likewise present dangers in unfamiliar business sectors. Issues, for example, work rehearses, common liberties concerns, and ecological maintainability are progressively significant contemplations for organizations. Organizations should adjust their tasks to nearby cultural assumptions and ecological guidelines to keep away from reaction from customers, financial backers, and administrative bodies.

International strains and exchange debates can fundamentally affect organizations working in unfamiliar business sectors. Abrupt changes in exchange strategies, duties, or political relations can upset supply chains and market access. Organizations need to remain informed about international turns of events and survey the expected effect on their activities. Creating adaptable techniques that can adjust to changing international scenes is urgent for relieving these dangers.

Mechanical difficulties, including network protection dangers, can likewise influence organizations in unfamiliar business sectors. As organizations become more dependent on advanced innovations, they become vulnerable to digital assaults, information breaks, and other mechanical dangers. Executing vigorous network safety gauges and remaining in front of mechanical progressions are fundamental for safeguarding delicate data and keeping up with the trust of clients and accomplices.

Social and political turmoil can establish an unpredictable business climate in unfamiliar business sectors. Fights, shows, or common turmoil can disturb typical business tasks and posture dangers for representatives and resources. Organizations should evaluate the international soundness of the districts they work in and have alternate courses of action set up to guarantee the security of their faculty and resources during times of social or political commotion.

Wellbeing and dangers, including pandemics and irresistible sicknesses, stand out enough to be noticed following the worldwide spread of Coronavirus. The pandemic showed the interconnectedness of the worldwide economy and the weakness of organizations to wellbeing related emergencies. Organizations need to integrate hearty wellbeing and security conventions into their tasks and inventory network the executives to moderate the effect of possible flare-ups.

In rundown, the dangers related with unfamiliar business sectors are multi-layered and require a far reaching risk the executives approach. Political flimsiness, monetary vulnerability, social contrasts, legitimate and administrative difficulties, market rivalry, framework issues, money and monetary dangers, licensed innovation assurance, inventory network interruptions, defilement, social and natural elements, international pressures, mechanical difficulties, social and political agitation, and wellbeing and dangers all add to the intricacy of carrying on with work universally.

Effective route of these dangers requires intensive examination, vital preparation, and progressing checking of the business climate. Organizations should likewise be versatile and receptive to changes, with the capacity to turn their systems in light of unexpected occasions. By getting it and proactively tending to these dangers, organizations can situate themselves for outcome in the dynamic and serious scene of unfamiliar business sectors.

Chapter 6

Building Strategic Partnerships

Building vital organizations is a critical part of business development and improvement in the present dynamic and interconnected worldwide scene. Organizations across ventures are progressively perceiving the worth of joint effort and collusions to improve their upper hand, drive advancement, and make practical progress. In this extensive investigation, we will dig into the complexities of building vital organizations, looking at the key standards, difficulties, and advantages related with manufacturing significant and commonly helpful unions.

At the center of building vital associations is the acknowledgment that no business works in segregation. In a period where markets are developing quickly, mechanical headways are speeding up, and customer assumptions are continually changing, associations should look for cooperative energies with outer elements to explore intricacies and take advantage of chances. Key organizations, when made with prescience and accuracy, can be extraordinary, impelling organizations higher than ever and encouraging flexibility notwithstanding vulnerabilities.

The commencement of an essential organization frequently starts with an essential aim, a reasonable comprehension of what each accomplice offers that would be useful, and a common vision for what's in store. Whether it's a joint endeavor, a cooperative exploration drive, or a provider client relationship, the arrangement of targets and values is vital. The distinguishing proof of integral qualities and capacities establishes the groundwork for an organization that isn't just powerful yet in addition equipped for enduring the unavoidable difficulties that might emerge.

In the domain of vital organizations, the advantages reach out a long ways past the prompt additions. While cost-sharing and chance alleviation are substantial benefits, the immaterial advantages of information trade, admittance to new business sectors, and improved brand notoriety are similarly huge. The cooperative endeavors of at least two elements can bring about collaborations that drive development, work with learning, and make an upper hand that would be trying to freely accomplish.

One of the essential standards in building vital associations is the requirement for compelling correspondence. Open and straightforward correspondence channels are fundamental to lay out trust and arrangement between accomplices. Standard updates, clear assumptions, and a common obligation to the organization's goals make a strong starting point for joint effort. This standard stretches out not exclusively to the underlying phases of association arrangement yet stays basic all through the organization's lifecycle.

Notwithstanding, viable correspondence is only one feature of fruitful association building. The cycle likewise requests a careful comprehension of each accomplice's hierarchical culture, values, and functional elements. Contrasts in hierarchical culture can be a wellspring of solidarity whenever oversaw accurately, carrying different points of view and ways to deal with critical thinking. In any case, on the off chance that not tended to proactively, these distinctions can become obstacles to joint effort, prompting erosion and at last imperiling the association.

Vital organizations are not without their difficulties. The potential for irreconcilable circumstances, contrasting assumptions, and the advancing idea of ventures can present critical obstacles. It is essential to proactively expect and address these difficulties. Laying out clear administration structures, characterizing jobs and obligations, and having components set up for compromise are fundamental components of powerful association the board.

Notwithstanding inner difficulties, outside elements like administrative changes, financial variances, and international occasions can influence the elements of an essential organization. Associations should be lithe and versatile, prepared to recalibrate their procedures and activities to explore the steadily changing outside scene. A versatile organization is one that can turn and develop because of both inward and outside impacts.

The determination of the right accomplice is a basic choice that can represent the deciding moment an essential union. A careful expected level of investment process is fundamental to evaluate the possible accomplice's monetary steadiness, notoriety, and arrangement with the association's qualities and goals. Past these primary rules, similarity regarding key vision, development capacities, and long haul objectives is vital for an organization to flourish.

When an essential organization is laid out, it requires progressing the board and supporting. Normal execution surveys, criticism instruments, and a guarantee to consistent improvement are fundamental components of organization administration. The capacity to adjust to evolving conditions, return to and change the association's objectives, and influence arising open doors is critical to guaranteeing the organization stays significant and effective over the long run.

With regards to building vital organizations, the innovation area has been a ripe ground for coordinated effort and development. The speedy idea of mechanical headways, combined with the intricacy of settling contemporary difficulties, has driven organizations to look for associations that influence the qualities of various substances. Cooperative endeavors in innovative work, joint endeavors, and environment organizations have become normal techniques for innovation organizations meaning to remain at the bleeding edge of development.

For instance, in the semiconductor business, where headways are basic for remaining cutthroat, key organizations empower organizations to pool assets for innovative work drives. This cooperative methodology speeds up the speed of development as well as permits organizations to share the significant expenses related with state of the art research.

By fashioning unions with correlative accomplices, semiconductor organizations can get to a more extensive scope of mastery and capacities, at last bringing about the improvement of additional vigorous and modern innovations.

In the medical care area, key organizations have become instrumental in tending to complex difficulties like medication disclosure, clinical preliminaries, and the advancement of creative treatments. Drug organizations frequently structure vital coalitions with biotechnology firms, research foundations, and different partners to consolidate their aptitude and assets. These organizations speed up the medication improvement process, improve the probability of fruitful results, and add to progressions in clinical science.

Past the confidential area, state run administrations and worldwide associations likewise perceive the significance of key organizations in tending to worldwide difficulties. Cooperative drives between nations, worldwide offices, and non-administrative associations are fundamental for handling issues, for example, environmental change, general wellbeing emergencies, and financial differences. The Unified Countries, for example, fills in as a stage for nations to frame partnerships and direction endeavors to resolve squeezing worldwide issues that rise above public boundaries.

While the advantages of vital organizations are apparent, it is fundamental to recognize the possible traps and dangers related with coordinated effort. One of the normal difficulties is the issue of licensed innovation (IP) insurance. At the point when at least two elements meet up to team up, there is a need to characterize how licensed innovation produced during the organization will be possessed, shared, and secured. Inability to address these worries forthright can prompt questions and lawful complexities down the line.

Besides, the social distinctions referenced before can appear in different ways, affecting correspondence as well as dynamic cycles and ways to deal with critical thinking. It is basic to put time and exertion in understanding and regarding the social subtleties of accomplice associations to cultivate a cooperative climate.

Monetary contemplations likewise assume a urgent part in the outcome of vital organizations. Issues connected with subsidizing, asset portion, and the dispersion of expenses and advantages can strain the organization in the event that not oversaw wisely. Accomplices should be straightforward about their monetary abilities and assumptions, guaranteeing that the organization stays impartial and valuable together.

One more test in building key organizations is the potential for misalignment in objectives and needs. Associations might go into organizations with various assumptions, and over the long haul, these assumptions might separate. Standard correspondence and a promise to return to and realign objectives are vital for address this test and guarantee that the organization stays zeroed in on shared targets.

Notwithstanding these difficulties, the speedy idea of business and mechanical headways requires a degree of dexterity and flexibility in essential organizations. An association manufactured considering a particular objective might have to develop as economic situations change, new open doors emerge, or unexpected difficulties arise. The capacity to turn and recalibrate techniques is significant for the drawn out supportability of the association.

Notwithstanding these difficulties, the expected prizes of key associations are too influential for even consider disregarding. Producing partnerships can open new business sectors, drive development, improve functional proficiency, and make an upper hand. Nonetheless, progress in building vital organizations requires a conscious and smart methodology from the beginning of the organization through its whole lifecycle.

To explore the intricacies of vital organizations effectively, associations can embrace an organized system that incorporates key phases of association improvement, execution, and the board. This structure fills in as a guide, directing associations through the complexities of joint effort and assisting them with boosting the advantages of their essential partnerships.

The principal phase of the association lifecycle is the ID and evaluation of likely accomplices. This includes a careful assessment of the essential scene, recognizing elements that have reciprocal qualities and capacities. Associations should consider factors like industry notoriety, monetary steadiness, social fit, and the potential for long haul cooperation. This expected level of effort process is urgent for choosing accomplices that line up with the association's objectives and values.

When potential accomplices are distinguished, the subsequent stage is to start conversations and talks. This stage includes characterizing the extension and goals of the organization, explaining assumptions, and laying out a strong starting point for cooperation. Clear correspondence is vital during this stage, as it establishes the vibe for the whole organization. Associations should guarantee that there is arrangement in essential vision, a common obligation to progress, and a shared comprehension of each party's jobs and obligations.

The formalization of the organization happens through the turn of events and consenting to of a far reaching arrangement. This arrangement frames the agreements of the association, including administration structures, dynamic cycles, and components for compromise. Legitimate and monetary contemplations are essential during this stage, and associations might look for lawful direction to guarantee that the understanding is hearty and defensive of their inclinations.

With the organization understanding set up, the execution stage starts. This includes the genuine execution of cooperative drives, whether it's joint innovative work, co-promoting endeavors, or shared assets.

Compelling task the board, normal correspondence, and a pledge to straightforwardness are fundamental during this stage. Associations should ceaselessly survey progress, address difficulties expeditiously, and guarantee that the organization conveys the expected advantages.

The administration and enhancement of the association comprise the continuous period of the lifecycle. Normal execution surveys, input systems, and assessments of the organization's effect are significant for its supported achievement. As economic situations advance and new open doors arise, associations should be deft and versatile, prepared to change their systems and recalibrate the organization to guarantee proceeded with importance and viability.

All through the organization lifecycle, viable correspondence stays a key part. Open and straightforward correspondence channels work with coordinated effort, construct trust, and add to the general progress of the association. Normal correspondence permits accomplices to remain informed about progress, difficulties, and changes in the outside climate, empowering them to settle on informed choices and changes.

Notwithstanding the lifecycle stages, certain prescribed procedures can improve the probability of progress in building vital associations. One such practice is the foundation of a devoted organization supervisory group. This group is answerable for administering the everyday exercises of the organization, working with correspondence among accomplices, and guaranteeing that the association stays lined up with its objectives.

Besides, associations ought to develop a culture of cooperation inside. This includes encouraging a climate where workers worth and embrace coordinated effort, perceiving its significance in driving development and accomplishing shared targets. At the point when representatives at all levels grasp the meaning of the organization and are lined up with its objectives, it adds to the association's general achievement.

Development is a critical driver of vital associations, and associations ought to effectively look for chances to improve cooperatively. This might include joint innovative work drives, the investigation of new business sectors, or the co-formation of items and administrations. By utilizing the aggregate qualities of the accomplices, associations can accomplish forward leaps that would be trying to freely achieve.

Estimating the outcome of an essential organization requires a blend of quantitative and subjective measurements. While monetary measurements, for example, profit from speculation and cost investment funds are significant, associations ought to likewise survey the organization's effect on development, market reach, and by and large intensity. Ordinary assessments in light of these measurements empower associations to come to educated conclusions about the future regarding the organization.

6.1 Importance of forming alliances with local partners

In the powerful scene of worldwide business, the significance of framing coalitions with nearby accomplices couldn't possibly be more significant. As associations endeavor to extend their impression and explore different business sectors, the job of neighborhood organizations turns into an essential objective. This thorough investigation digs into the complex purposes for the meaning of developing collusions with nearby accomplices, analyzing the benefits, difficulties, and key contemplations related with this essential methodology.

Market Knowledge and Understanding:

One of the essential purposes behind shaping collusions with neighborhood accomplices is acquiring important bits of knowledge into the subtleties of the nearby market. Neighborhood accomplices bring an inside and out comprehension of the social, monetary, and administrative scene. This information is instrumental in fitting items and administrations to meet the particular requirements and inclinations of the neighborhood populace. Whether it's grasping shopper conduct, exploring administrative necessities, or adjusting showcasing systems, neighborhood accomplices act as significant aides, giving a nuanced point of view that can be provoking for outside elements to freely accomplish.

Exploring Social Intricacy:

Social subtleties assume a crucial part in the achievement or disappointment of organizations in unfamiliar business sectors. Neighborhood accomplices, being imbued in the nearby culture, offer an extension that assists associations with exploring the mind boggling trap of social complexities. From correspondence styles and accepted practices to business behavior, nearby accomplices act as social mediators, guaranteeing that the association's methodology isn't just conscious yet in addition resounds with the neighborhood crowd. This social familiarity is basic in building trust, encouraging positive connections, and laying out a significant presence in the neighborhood local area.

Laying out Believability and Trust:

Believability is a cash that holds enormous worth in the business world, particularly in new domains. Nearby accomplices, with their laid out organizations and notoriety inside the local area, give a pivotal underwriting to the entering association. This current validity loans an atmosphere of trust, working with smoother communications with nearby partners, including clients, providers, and administrative specialists. The underwriting from a regarded nearby accomplice can essentially decrease wariness and obstruction that unfamiliar substances could experience in another market.

Utilizing Nearby Organizations:

Building an organization without any preparation in another market can be a tedious and testing try. Neighborhood accomplices, with their prior organizations, offer an easy route to laying out essential associations.

Whether it's structure associations with key providers, wholesalers, or persuasive figures locally, nearby accomplices bring an abundance of associations that can facilitate the course of incorporation into the neighborhood business biological system. This organization impact speeds up market section as well as opens ways to open doors that could have stayed subtle without nearby experiences.

Administrative Consistence and Nearby Aptitude:

Exploring the maze of administrative necessities in an unfamiliar market can be an overwhelming errand. Neighborhood accomplices, knowledgeable in the nearby administrative scene, give a directing hand to guarantee consistence with regulations and guidelines. From permitting and allows to understanding duty structures, a nearby accomplice's skill can forestall exorbitant slips up and legitimate confusions. Their experience with the administrative cycles smoothes out activities, permitting the entering association to zero in on its center abilities while depending on the neighborhood accomplice's information to actually explore administrative complexities.

Risk Relief:

Worldwide extension intrinsically implies a degree of chance, going from administrative vulnerabilities to showcase elements. Framing unions with nearby accomplices fills in as a gamble relief technique. By imparting the dangers and obligations to a believed nearby substance, associations can fence against the vulnerabilities related with entering another market. This cooperative methodology guarantees that the association isn't exploring a strange area alone, utilizing the neighborhood accomplice's insight and experiences to relieve dangers and improve the probability of progress.

Cost Effectiveness and Asset Improvement:

Laying out a presence in an unfamiliar market without any preparation requests huge monetary and HR. Neighborhood accomplices can give a savvy elective by sharing the monetary weight and utilizing their current foundation. This is especially pertinent in areas where actual presence, for example, circulation organizations or retail outlets, is fundamental. Neighborhood accomplices add to asset enhancement, permitting the entering association to distribute assets decisively, zeroing in on regions where its center capabilities are generally required.

Variation to Nearby Inclinations:

Purchaser inclinations can fluctuate generally across various districts, and what works in a single market may not be guaranteed to resound in another. Neighborhood accomplices bring a profound comprehension of buyer conduct, inclinations, and patterns in their home market. This understanding is important for modifying items, administrations, and promoting systems to line up with nearby preferences. By adjusting to neighborhood inclinations, associations can situate themselves all the more really on the lookout, improving the probability of acknowledgment and long haul achievement.

Upper hand Through Neighborhood Experiences:

In the worldwide field, rivalry is furious, and acquiring an upper hand requires a nuanced comprehension of the market. Neighborhood accomplices give an upper hand by offering experiences into the techniques and strategies of nearby contenders. This information empowers associations to tweak their market situating, separate themselves actually, and foster techniques that exploit the shortcomings or holes in the contributions of contenders. By utilizing nearby experiences, associations can figure out additional educated and designated ways to deal with gain an upper hand.

Quicker Market Infiltration:

Speed is frequently of the embodiment in the business world, and framing unions with neighborhood accomplices works with quicker market entrance. The neighborhood accomplice's current framework, dispersion channels, and market presence give an early advantage, empowering the entering association to quickly lay out a traction more. This facilitated market passage is especially profitable in businesses where being an early participant can convert into a maintainable upper hand.

Challenges in Shaping Coalitions with Nearby Accomplices:

While the advantages of shaping collusions with neighborhood accomplices are significant, it is fundamental to recognize and explore the difficulties related with this essential methodology. One normal test is tracking down the right nearby accomplice. The determination interaction requires cautious thought of elements like similarity, shared values, and arrangement of key objectives. Inability to pick the right accomplice can prompt befuddles in assumptions, social conflicts, and, at last, the disappointment of the coalition.

Social contrasts, notwithstanding being a wellspring of significant experiences, can likewise present difficulties. Miscommunication, misconceptions, and varying ways to deal with business tasks might emerge in the event that social subtleties are not overseen actually. Putting time and exertion in social responsiveness preparing and encouraging open correspondence channels are crucial for address these difficulties and guarantee an amicable and useful organization.

One more potential test is keeping an overall influence in the collusion. Variations in size, assets, or impact between the entering association and the neighborhood accomplice can prompt uneven characters, influencing dynamic cycles and the general elements of the organization. Laying out clear administration structures, characterized jobs, and open correspondence are crucial to relieve the gamble of force irregular characteristics and guarantee a cooperative and commonly useful organization.

Licensed innovation (IP) security is a basic worry in global joint efforts. Imparting restrictive data to a neighborhood accomplice implies the gamble of unapproved use or replication. Executing powerful legitimate arrangements, obviously illustrating IP

EXPORT STRATEGIES

possession and use freedoms, is fundamental to safeguard the entering association's scholarly resources.

Carefulness and proactive measures are important to forestall potential IP-related debates that could endanger the outcome of the collusion.

The steadily changing international scene adds one more layer of intricacy to shaping collusions with neighborhood accomplices. Political precariousness, exchange strains, or changes in government approaches can affect the administrative climate and business conditions. Associations should direct intensive gamble evaluations and keep up to date with international improvements to expect and answer actually to potential provokes that might emerge because of outside factors.

Systems for Fruitful Coalitions with Neighborhood Accomplices:

Exploring the difficulties of shaping unions with neighborhood accomplices requires a smart and key methodology. A few key procedures can improve the probability of progress and add to the life span and viability of the organization.

Intensive Reasonable level of investment:

The groundwork of a fruitful coalition is based on exhaustive expected level of effort in the determination of a nearby accomplice. Associations should lead extensive appraisals of likely accomplices, taking into account factors, for example, their monetary strength, notoriety, history, and arrangement with the association's qualities. Site visits, interviews, and an itemized examination of the accomplice's capacities are fundamental parts of the expected level of investment process.

Clear Correspondence and Assumptions:

Open and straightforward correspondence is the foundation of fruitful organizations. Obviously characterizing assumptions, jobs, and obligations from the beginning forestalls misconceptions and adjusts the two players towards shared objectives. Standard correspondence channels, criticism systems, and continuous discourse add to a cooperative and responsive organization.

Social Responsiveness and Preparing:

Proactively tending to social contrasts is essential for encouraging an agreeable organization. Social responsiveness preparing for workers engaged with the collusion can upgrade culturally diverse correspondence and understanding. Building a culture of regard for variety and inclusivity inside the association adds to a positive and cooperative climate.

Adjusted Power Elements:

Moderating power irregular characteristics requires the foundation of adjusted administration structures. Obviously characterized dynamic cycles, straightforward correspondence, and instruments for compromise add to a more evenhanded dispersion of force inside the partnership. Ordinary assessments of the organization's elements can help distinguish and address potential irregular characteristics speedily.

Far reaching Legitimate Arrangements:

Hearty legitimate arrangements are fundamental to safeguard the interests of the two players. Agreements ought to obviously frame the particulars of the partnership, including administration structures, IP proprietorship, question goal systems, and leave procedures. Legitimate direction with mastery in global associations can give important direction in creating arrangements that are lawfully strong and defensive of the two players.

Nonstop Observing and Variation:

The business climate is dynamic, and effective partnerships require consistent checking and variation. Normal execution surveys, appraisals of economic situations, and assessments of the association's effect add to informed navigation. The capacity to adjust methodologies, return to objectives, and make vital changes guarantees that the partnership stays significant and successful after some time.

Interest in Relationship Building:

Building solid connections is a drawn out interest in the progress of the coalition. Past conventional arrangements and deals, putting resources into relationship building encourages trust and coordinated effort. Up close and personal cooperations, joint exercises, and social commitment add to the improvement of a positive and persevering through organization.

Risk Alleviation Procedures:

Proactively recognizing and relieving chances is an essential basic in global collusions. Associations ought to foster gamble alleviation procedures that envelop different situations, remembering changes for administrative conditions, international movements, and financial vacillations. Having alternate courses of action set up guarantees a more spry and strong reaction to unexpected difficulties.

Shared Vision and Values:

Arrangement in vision and values is a fundamental component of effective organizations. Associations ought to look for accomplices whose goals and values line up with their own. A common vision makes serious areas of strength for a for coordinated effort, cultivating a feeling of direction and responsibility that adds to the general progress of the coalition.

6.2 Types of strategic partnerships: joint ventures, distributorships, licensing

In the domain of key business drives, framing organizations is a foundation technique for associations looking for development, market extension, and upgraded capacities. Inside the expansive range of key associations, three conspicuous sorts — joint endeavors, distributorships, and authorizing arrangements — stick out, each offering novel benefits and contemplations. This investigation digs into the complexities of these essential organization models, inspecting their qualities, advantages, difficulties, and key contemplations for execution.

Joint Endeavors:

A joint endeavor (JV) addresses a cooperative exertion between at least two substances to make a new, imparted element to a particular business objective. In a joint endeavor, partaking associations pool their assets, mastery, and money to seek after a shared objective while keeping up with their singular personalities. JVs are portrayed by shared possession, shared chances, and shared rewards, making them a unique vehicle for entering new business sectors, sending off inventive ventures, or consolidating corresponding capacities.

One of the vital benefits of joint endeavors is the capacity to use the qualities of each accomplice. By uniting different aptitude, assets, and points of view, associations can accomplish collaborations that may be trying to freely achieve. This cooperative methodology cultivates development, speeds up market section, and frequently brings about a more strong and tough business substance.

Joint endeavors are especially common in ventures where critical capital speculations, particular information, or administrative consistence are fundamental. For instance, in the energy area, oil and gas organizations frequently structure joint dares to share the significant expenses and dangers related with investigation and advancement projects. By consolidating monetary assets and specialized mastery, accomplices can embrace aggressive drives that might be past the extent of individual associations.

While joint endeavors offer convincing benefits, they likewise accompany intrinsic difficulties. Compelling correspondence and navigation are basic parts of a fruitful JV. Accomplices should explore shared administration structures, distribute liabilities, and lay out systems for settling questions. The potential for irreconcilable circumstances or contrasts in essential vision requires proactive administration to guarantee a firm and commonly useful association.

Moreover, social arrangement is principal in joint endeavors including substances from various locales or foundations. Differences in authoritative culture, the board styles, and strategic approaches can affect the outcome of the joint effort. Building a common culture and cultivating open correspondence channels are significant for beating social boundaries and making an amicable working relationship inside the joint endeavor.

Lawful contemplations likewise assume a focal part in joint endeavors. Creating a vigorous joint endeavor understanding that portrays the privileges, obligations, and leave systems is fundamental for relieving chances. Clear arrangements with respect to benefit dispersion, dynamic cycles, and question goal components add to the steadiness and life span of the joint endeavor.

Distributorships:

Distributorships involve an essential association where one substance, known as the merchant, takes on the obligation of showcasing, selling, and frequently overhauling the items or administrations of another element, the maker or maker. This sort of association is predominant across different ventures, including purchaser merchandise, innovation, and modern items. Distributorships are instrumental in extending market reach, taking advantage of laid out appropriation channels, and profiting from the nearby information and market mastery of the conveyance accomplice.

One of the essential benefits of distributorships is the sped up market passage they offer. Rather than exploring the intricacies of setting up and dealing with an immediate deals power or dispersion organization, associations can use the current foundation and capacities of the wholesaler. This outcomes in quicker market entrance and admittance to a more extensive client base, particularly in districts where the wholesaler as of now has major areas of strength for a.

Distributorships additionally give cost efficiencies to the two players. Makers can zero in on their center abilities, like item advancement and development, while merchants handle the complexities of deals, planned operations, and client assistance. Wholesalers, thusly, benefit from laid out brand value and the potential for expanded incomes through the offer of integral items.

In any case, challenges in distributorships rotate around keeping up with arrangement in essential targets, brand portrayal, and client assistance guidelines. While merchants work autonomously, their activities straightforwardly influence the standing of the maker. Clear correspondence, preparing projects, and ordinary execution assessments are significant to guaranteeing that the merchant lines up with the producer's image picture and values.

Overseeing associations with various wholesalers can represent extra difficulties. In situations where a producer draws in with numerous wholesalers across different districts, keeping up with consistency in informing, estimating, and administration levels turns into a perplexing errand. Vital coordination and successful correspondence are fundamental to orchestrate endeavors and guarantee a durable brand presence in different business sectors.

To alleviate the dangers related with distributorships, producers should lead exhaustive reasonable level of effort in choosing appropriation accomplices. Surveying the merchant's market information, monetary security, and obligation to the brand is basic. Laying out legally binding arrangements that obviously frame assumptions, regions, and execution measurements adds to a more organized and responsible organization.

Permitting Arrangements:

Permitting arrangements address an essential association model where one party (the licensor) awards another party (the licensee) the privileges to utilize, produce, or sell its protected innovation, like licenses, brand names, copyrights, or exclusive innovation. Authorizing arrangements are adaptable and find application across ventures going from innovation and amusement to purchaser products. This kind of association permits associations to adapt their scholarly resources, extend market presence, and tap into new income streams.

The essential benefit of permitting arrangements is the capacity to use protected innovation without the requirement for huge capital speculation or functional contribution. For licensors, permitting gives a way to create income from their scholarly resources while relieving the dangers and expenses related with assembling and dissemination. Licensees, then again, get to laid out brands, innovations, or content without the need to foster these resources without any preparation.

Permitting arrangements are especially predominant in media outlets, where film studios permit characters, establishments, or product freedoms to create extra income streams. Essentially, in the innovation area, organizations might permit their protected advances to outsiders, considering more extensive market reception while getting eminences for the utilization of their developments.

In any case, the progress of authorizing arrangements depends on clear conditions and conditions that safeguard the interests of the two players. Licensors should characterize the extent of the permit, limitations on use, and the span of the understanding. Eminence designs and installment terms ought to be straightforward, and components for observing and authorizing the permit should be set up to protect the licensor's licensed innovation.

Guaranteeing consistence with permitting terms can be a mind boggling try, particularly in peaceful accords where lawful systems and requirement components might change. Licensors should direct expected level of effort to comprehend the lawful scene of the regions wherein the permit will be implemented, and licensees should comply to authoritative commitments to keep away from legitimate repercussions.

One test in permitting arrangements is the potential for irreconcilable situations. Licensees might have disparate business methodologies or market needs that influence the licensor's image or protected innovation. Keeping a harmony between the licensor's assumptions and the licensee's business targets requires progressing correspondence and coordinated effort.

Moreover, the gamble of unapproved use or encroachment by outsiders represents a worry in permitting plans. Licensors should execute powerful checking components to quickly recognize and address occurrences of unapproved use. Legitimate plan of action and implementation measures ought to be obviously characterized in the consent to safeguard the licensor's protected innovation privileges.

Key Contemplations for Execution:

No matter what the sort of essential association — joint endeavors, distributorships, or permitting arrangements — effective execution requires cautious thought of different variables. A few key contemplations can direct associations in exploring the intricacies and expanding the advantages of these organizations.

Key Arrangement:

Prior to setting out on an essential association, associations should evaluate the essential arrangement between expected accomplices. Whether it's a joint endeavor, distributorship, or permitting arrangement, shared objectives, values, and a common comprehension of each party's commitments and assumptions are basic to progress. A misalignment in essential targets can prompt contentions and thwart the accomplishment of shared objectives.

A reasonable level of investment:

Careful expected level of effort is basic in choosing the right accomplices for an essential partnership. Associations should assess the monetary solidness, notoriety, and abilities of possible accomplices. On account of joint endeavors, seeing each accomplice's history, mastery, and social similarity is essential. For distributorships, surveying the conveyance accomplice's market information, reach, and obligation to mark portrayal is fundamental. Permitting arrangements require an extensive assessment of the licensor's protected innovation and the licensee's capacity to stick to legally binding commitments.

Clear Correspondence:

Powerful correspondence is a key part in any essential organization. Open and straightforward correspondence channels should be laid out from the beginning and kept up with all through the organization's lifecycle. Clear verbalization of assumptions, jobs, and obligations is fundamental to keep away from misconceptions and encourage a cooperative climate. Normal correspondence helps in tending to difficulties speedily and guarantees that the two players stay lined up with the organization's goals.

Lawful System:

A strong legitimate system is basic for the achievement and supportability of any essential organization. Lawful arrangements should be exhaustive, obviously illustrating the agreements overseeing the union. Whether it's a joint endeavor understanding, a distributorship contract, or a permitting arrangement, the legitimate system ought to address administration structures, dynamic cycles, question goal components, and leave techniques. Lawful advice with mastery in the particular kind of organization can give significant direction in making arrangements that are legitimately solid and defensive of the two players.

Risk Relief:

Risk alleviation methodologies ought to be a fundamental piece of the organization arranging process. Associations should expect likely dangers, whether they connect with market elements, administrative changes, social contrasts, or licensed innovation assurance.

Creating emergency courses of action, directing situation investigations, and carrying out checking systems add to a more light-footed and strong organization.

Social Responsiveness:

Social responsiveness is especially pertinent in worldwide associations or those including substances from assorted foundations. Understanding and regarding social subtleties add to powerful correspondence, relationship building, and generally coordinated effort. Preparing projects and drives that advance social mindfulness can upgrade the progress of the organization by limiting errors and cultivating a positive working relationship.

Execution Measurements:

Laying out clear execution measurements and key execution markers (KPIs) is fundamental for estimating the progress of the organization. Whether it's assessing the monetary exhibition of a joint endeavor, observing deals and conveyance measurements in a distributorship, or evaluating sovereignty installments in a permitting understanding, having quantifiable benchmarks gives a premise to execution surveys and acclimations to the association procedure.

Adaptability and Flexibility:

The business climate is dynamic, and organizations should be adaptable and versatile to evolving conditions. Whether it's moving economic situations, mechanical headways, or developing purchaser inclinations, associations should be ready to recalibrate their techniques, return to objectives, and make fundamental acclimations to guarantee the organization stays significant and successful after some time.

6.3 Showcasing successful collaboration models

In the steadily developing scene of business, effective coordinated effort models stand as models of how associations can use organizations to accomplish shared objectives, drive advancement, and upgrade their upper hand. These models feature the force of joint effort in different structures, showing how assorted substances, from industry pioneers to new businesses and exploration establishments, can meet up to make cooperative energies that push them higher than ever. This investigation digs into a few effective coordinated effort models, inspecting their key qualities, benefits, and the examples they offer for associations looking to produce significant organizations.

Open Advancement Biological systems:

Open development biological systems address a cooperative model where associations team up across customary limits to share thoughts, assets, and mastery. Not at all like shut advancement models, which depend on inner innovative work, open development environments embrace outside cooperation, taking advantage of an organization of accomplices, new companies, and exploration establishments. This model cultivates a climate where thoughts stream unreservedly, and members all in all add to settling complex difficulties.

One praiseworthy occurrence of an open development biological system is the MIT Media Lab. The MIT Media Lab fills in as a multidisciplinary center where scientists, specialists, creators, and industry accomplices combine to investigate state of the art advances and their likely applications. The lab's open advancement approach supports joint effort among the scholarly world and industry, prompting momentous developments in fields like man-made consciousness, human-PC cooperation, and media expressions.

The advantages of open advancement environments are complex. Members get close enough to a different pool of mastery, permitting them to handle difficulties according to different viewpoints. The liquid trade of thoughts and information speeds up the speed of advancement, prompting the improvement of arrangements that might not have been imaginable inside the bounds of a solitary association. For industry accomplices, drawing in with open development biological systems gives an upper hand by remaining at the cutting edge of arising advances and patterns.

Key to the outcome of open development biological systems is a culture of receptiveness, joint effort, and information sharing. Trust among members is principal, as they explore the intricacies of licensed innovation, information sharing, and cooperative navigation. Clear administration structures, straightforward correspondence channels, and distinct systems for perceiving and remunerating commitments guarantee that the environment stays dynamic and useful.

Industry-The scholarly community Joint efforts:

The coordinated effort among ventures and scholarly foundations is a strong model that has filled advancement developments and progressions across different areas. This coordinated effort model normally includes associations among organizations and colleges or exploration foundations, where industry accomplices benefit from admittance to state of the art examination, and scholastic establishments gain genuine applications for their examination discoveries.

A striking illustration of fruitful industry-the scholarly community cooperation is the organization among IBM and MIT for the MIT-IBM Watson computer based intelligence Lab. This joint effort unites IBM's mastery in computerized reasoning and MIT's scholastic ability to propel man-made intelligence research, foster new advancements, and train the up and coming age of simulated intelligence experts. The lab's emphasis on crucial simulated intelligence research, as well as its obligation to tending to the cultural ramifications of computer based intelligence, represents the profundity and effect feasible through industry-the scholarly community cooperation.

The benefits of industry-the scholarly community coordinated efforts are multilayered. Organizations get to the most recent examination, particular information, and arising ability, empowering them to remain on the ball in quickly advancing enterprises.

Scholastic establishments, thusly, get financing, genuine applications for their exploration, and open doors for their staff and understudies to draw in with industry challenges. This cooperative relationship makes a unique environment where hypothetical bits of knowledge are converted into reasonable arrangements.

Challenges in industry-the scholarly community joint efforts frequently rotate around contrasts in authoritative societies, courses of events, and goals. Industry accomplices might focus on transient objectives and commonsense applications, while the scholarly community will in general accentuate long haul research and hypothetical headways. Powerful correspondence, shared understanding, and the foundation of clear assumptions add to defeating these difficulties and encouraging fruitful joint efforts.

Key Partnerships in the Drug Business:

The drug business is described by complex examination processes, rigid administrative necessities, and the requirement for significant interests in drug improvement.

In this specific circumstance, key collusions have arisen as a fruitful coordinated effort model, empowering drug organizations to pool assets, share chances, and facilitate the disclosure and improvement of new treatments.

A convincing model is the essential collusion among AstraZeneca and Oxford College for the turn of events and conveyance of the Coronavirus immunization. This coordinated effort exhibited the force of uniting scholastic examination, drug mastery, and assembling capacities to address a worldwide wellbeing emergency. By utilizing each other's assets, AstraZeneca and Oxford College sped up the timetable for antibody improvement and dissemination.

Vital collusions in the drug business offer a few benefits. They empower organizations to share the significant expenses and dangers related with drug improvement, access integral skill, and grow their pipelines. For scholarly organizations, these unions give subsidizing, admittance to industry bits of knowledge, and chances to make an interpretation of examination discoveries into substantial restorative arrangements.

Exploring the intricacies of key unions in the drug business requires cautious thought of protected innovation, administrative consistence, and administration structures. Clear settlements on the freedoms to created treatments, the sharing of advancement expenses, and dynamic cycles are basic for the outcome of these joint efforts. Compelling task the board and straightforward correspondence guarantee that the partnership stays zeroed in on its goals and conveys ideal outcomes.

Cross-Industry Development Stages:

Cross-industry development stages unite associations from different areas to team up on settling normal difficulties or investigating new open doors. These stages work with the trading of thoughts, skill, and assets among members from various businesses, cultivating a cross-fertilization of experiences that can prompt novel arrangements and problematic developments.

One striking model is the Versatility Open Blockchain Drive (MOBI), a cooperation stage that unites car makers, innovation organizations, and blockchain specialists to investigate the capability of blockchain innovation in the portability area. Members in MOBI team up on projects connected with shrewd versatility, production network straightforwardness, and information sharing, expecting to make norms and arrangements that benefit the whole business.

The strength of cross-industry development stages lies in the variety of viewpoints they bring to critical thinking. By separating storehouses and empowering cooperation between areas, these stages advance inventiveness and the investigation of unusual thoughts. Members can use aptitude from different ventures, recognize shared difficulties, and aggregately foster arrangements that have more extensive applications.

Challenges in cross-industry advancement stages frequently spin around contrasts in phrasing, needs, and plans of action across areas. Powerful help, normal systems, and a common obligation to the general objectives of the stage add to beating these difficulties. Moreover, a culture of receptiveness to different viewpoints and a readiness to embrace trial and error are fundamental for the outcome of such coordinated efforts.

Worldwide Exploration Consortia:

Worldwide examination consortia address cooperative models where associations from around the world unite to address complex difficulties or seek after huge scope research drives. These consortia frequently include scholarly establishments, research associations, and industry accomplices cooperating on projects that require a worldwide point of view, significant assets, and different mastery.

A commendable case is the Human Genome Venture (HGP), a worldwide examination consortium sent off during the 1990s determined to plan and sequencing the whole human genome. This aggressive drive united researchers, analysts, and organizations from numerous nations, stamping quite possibly of the main cooperative exertion throughout the entire existence of genomics. The finish of the HGP gave a far reaching comprehension of the human genome and established the groundwork for headways in hereditary qualities, medication, and biotechnology.

The advantages of worldwide exploration consortia are broad. By pooling assets and ability from assorted districts, these joint efforts empower the handling of difficulties that outperform the capacities of individual associations or nations. Shared information, framework, and information speed up the speed of exploration and add to cutting edge disclosures with worldwide ramifications.

Notwithstanding, organizing worldwide exploration consortia presents special difficulties, remembering contrasts for guidelines, moral contemplations, and social standards. Laying out normalized conventions, guaranteeing information protection and security, and exploring global legitimate systems are basic parts of dealing with these coordinated efforts.

Clear correspondence, agreement building, and a promise to shared objectives add to the outcome of worldwide examination consortia.

Illustrations Learned and Best Practices:

The outcome of these coordinated effort models gives important illustrations and best practices for associations considering or participated in associations. A few overall topics rise up out of these effective joint efforts:

Shared Vision and Objectives:

Effective coordinated efforts are based on a common vision and objectives. Members should adjust on the general goals of the coordinated effort, whether it's propelling exploration, tending to a worldwide test, or making creative arrangements. An unmistakable and convincing shared vision gives a bringing together power that directs the cooperation's endeavors.

Clear Administration and Navigation:

Laying out clear administration designs and dynamic cycles is fundamental for the smooth working of joint efforts. Whether it's a joint endeavor, industry-the scholarly world association, or worldwide exploration consortium, members should characterize how choices will be made, how assets will be designated, and the way that clashes will be settled.

Open Correspondence and Straightforwardness:

Open correspondence and straightforwardness are central to fruitful coordinated efforts. Members should establish a climate where data streams unreservedly, thoughts are shared straightforwardly, and challenges are tended to straightforwardly. Customary correspondence channels, input systems, and gatherings for conversation add to a culture of receptiveness.

Social Responsiveness and Inclusivity:

Social responsiveness is significant in coordinated efforts including assorted substances. Perceiving and regarding social contrasts, whether they are hierarchical or provincial, encourages a comprehensive climate. Preparing programs, social trade drives, and variety and incorporation endeavors add to a cooperative culture that values alternate points of view.

Powerful Task The board:

Fruitful joint efforts require compelling venture the board to guarantee that objectives are met inside laid out timetables. Clear venture plans, achievements, and responsibility components add to the productive execution of cooperative drives. Project chiefs assume a basic part in organizing endeavors, overseeing assets, and keeping the cooperation on target.

Common Trust and Regard:

Trust is a foundation of effective coordinated efforts. Members should develop common trust by following through on responsibilities, regarding each other's commitments, and showing uprightness in their associations. Trust frames the establishment for versatile coordinated efforts that can weather conditions difficulties and adjust to evolving conditions.

Adaptability and Flexibility:

Joint effort models should be adaptable and versatile to advancing conditions. Whether it's moving economic situations, changes in administrative conditions, or surprising difficulties, members should be ready to change procedures, return to objectives, and make fundamental transformations. A readiness to embrace change and gain from encounters adds to the manageability of coordinated efforts.

Key Choice of Accomplices:

The progress of coordinated efforts frequently depends on the essential determination of accomplices. Whether shaping a joint endeavor, participating in an industry-the scholarly community cooperation, or partaking in a cross-industry development stage, associations should direct exhaustive reasonable level of effort to guarantee similarity in objectives, values, and capacities. Choosing accomplices with reciprocal qualities improves the probability of progress.

Interest in Relationship Building:

Building solid connections is a drawn out interest in the progress of joint efforts. Past proper arrangements and deals, putting resources into relationship building encourages trust, understanding, and a feeling of shared responsibility. Eye to eye associations, joint exercises, and social commitment add to the advancement of positive and getting through organizations.

Persistent Assessment and Improvement:

Joint efforts should go through constant assessment to evaluate their effect and viability. Standard execution surveys, criticism instruments, and assessments in light of predefined measurements give experiences into the cooperation's assets and regions for development. A promise to consistent learning and improvement adds to the life span and outcome of joint efforts.

Chapter 7

Logistics and Supply Chain Management

Strategies and Store network The board (SCM) assume essential parts in the progress of organizations across different enterprises. These interconnected disciplines include the coordination and advancement of cycles connected with the development and capacity of labor and products, from the starting place to the mark of utilization. In the present complex and globalized business climate, viable coordinated factors and production network the executives are basic for associations trying to upgrade effectiveness, diminish expenses, and gain an upper hand.

One essential part of coordinated factors is transportation, which envelops the actual development of merchandise starting with one area then onto the next. Proficient transportation frameworks are vital for limiting lead times, decreasing conveying costs, and guaranteeing convenient conveyance to clients. Whether merchandise are moved by street, rail, air, or ocean, choosing the proper method of transportation relies upon variables like the idea of the items, distance, cost contemplations, and speed necessities.

As of late, progressions in innovation have essentially affected coordinated operations and store network the board. The coordination of advanced innovations, like Web of Things (IoT), man-made consciousness (artificial intelligence), and blockchain, has changed the manner in which associations deal with their stock chains. IoT gadgets, for instance, give constant information on the area and state of merchandise during travel, empowering better perceivability and command over the production network.

Also, man-made intelligence fueled investigation assist associations with examining tremendous measures of information to recognize patterns, gauge interest, and improve stock levels. Prescient examination, specifically, has turned into an important device for expecting future interest designs and changing store network techniques likewise. By utilizing these advances, organizations can upgrade dynamic cycles, decrease functional shortcomings, and at last further develop by and large inventory network execution.

The idea of inventory network the executives includes an all encompassing way to deal with the whole interaction, from obtainment to creation and circulation. Key acquirement is imperative for getting the important unrefined substances and parts at the right expense and quality.

Associations frequently lay areas of strength for out with providers, taking part in cooperative endeavors to upgrade effectiveness and guarantee a steady stockpile of data sources.

Inventory network perceivability, another significant angle, includes following and observing the development of products at each stage. This straightforwardness permits organizations to recognize likely bottlenecks, relieve chances, and answer speedily to disturbances. Perceivability is especially basic in ventures where request is profoundly factor or where the production network traverses various nations and areas.

Distribution center administration is a necessary part of production network coordinated operations, zeroing in on the effective stockpiling and treatment of stock. The essential situation of stockrooms can fundamentally affect dispersion proficiency. Current stockrooms consolidate mechanization and advanced mechanics to smooth out processes, lessen blunders, and upgrade by and large functional proficiency.

Compelling stock administration is a difficult exercise that includes keeping up with ideal stock levels to fulfill client need while limiting conveying costs. In the nick of time (JIT) stock frameworks mean to limit stock holding costs by guaranteeing that merchandise show up precisely when required in the creation cycle. Nonetheless, JIT frameworks require exact coordination and can pretty much rule out blunder, making them defenseless to interruptions.

The globalization of supply chains enjoys the two benefits and difficulties. On one hand, it opens up new business sectors and permits organizations to source sources of info and parts from various locales, frequently at lower costs. Then again, worldwide stockpile fastens are powerless to international dangers, exchange debates, and catastrophic events that can disturb the progression of merchandise. The Coronavirus pandemic featured the weaknesses of worldwide stockpile chains, inciting associations to rethink their procedures and consider reshoring or nearshoring choices.

Risk the board is an essential piece of strategies and store network the executives. Associations should distinguish and evaluate expected gambles, foster alternate courses of action, and lay out strong store network organizations. This incorporates assessing the monetary steadiness of providers, surveying international dangers, and taking into account the effect of cataclysmic events or other unanticipated occasions.

The significance of manageability in strategies and production network the board has acquired noticeable quality lately. Reasonable practices add to natural preservation as well as line up with purchaser inclinations for eco-accommodating items and moral strategic policies. Organizations are progressively taking on maintainable obtaining, decreasing fossil fuel byproducts in transportation, and executing eco-accommodating bundling arrangements as a feature of their production network techniques.

Joint effort and correspondence are fundamental components of successful production network the board. In a universally scattered production network, coordination between different partners, including providers, makers, wholesalers, and retailers, is urgent. Correspondence innovations and coordinated effort stages work with continuous data sharing, empowering a more responsive and nimble store network.

The idea of the "request driven inventory network" underscores the significance of adjusting inventory network exercises to genuine client interest. By intently checking market patterns and client inclinations, associations can change creation plans, stock levels, and conveyance procedures to fulfill changing need designs. This client driven approach decreases the gamble of overloading or stockouts, improving by and large production network responsiveness.

Key production network configuration includes deciding the ideal construction of the inventory network organization. This incorporates choices in regards to the number and area of offices, transportation courses, and stock arrangement. A very much planned store network considers factors, for example, cost, administration levels, and adaptability, expecting to accomplish an equilibrium that meets both client and hierarchical targets.

In the period of online business, the elements of store network the executives have gone through huge changes. The ascent of online retail has prompted expanded assumptions for quick and solid conveyance. Web based business organizations should configuration supply anchors that take care of the remarkable requests of online customers, including last-mile conveyance contemplations, returns the board, and request satisfaction productivity.

Switch coordinated factors, the method involved with overseeing item returns and reusing, has turned into a basic part of inventory network the executives. As buyers progressively request bother free return processes, associations should foster productive converse operations methodologies to limit costs and natural effect. This includes carrying out powerful merchandise exchanges, reusing programs, and restoring drives.

The job of information examination in production network the board couldn't possibly be more significant. The accessibility of huge datasets gives chances to acquire experiences into different parts of the production network, from interest estimating to execution checking. Information driven direction empowers associations to distinguish shortcomings, streamline processes, and ceaselessly further develop store network execution.

Administrative consistence is a critical thought in strategies and store network the executives. Organizations working in various districts or nations should explore a complicated snare of guidelines connected with customs, exchange, and transportation. Resistance can bring about postponements, fines, and reputational harm, making it basic for associations to keep up to date with administrative necessities and guarantee adherence.

7.1 Efficient supply chain management in international trade

Effective store network the executives in worldwide exchange is a basic variable that can fundamentally influence the achievement and seriousness of organizations working on a worldwide scale. As associations grow their span across borders, they experience a horde of difficulties connected with coordinated factors, guidelines, social contrasts, and differing market elements. Really dealing with the development of merchandise, data, and funds across global limits is fundamental for enhancing activities, diminishing expenses, and meeting client assumptions.

One of the vital components in worldwide store network the executives is the essential choice of transportation modes. The decision between air, ocean, street, or rail transport relies upon elements like the idea of the items, time awareness, cost contemplations, and the geological distance between exchanging accomplices. Air transportation is frequently preferred for time-delicate and high-esteem merchandise, offering fast conveyance yet at a greater expense. Ocean transport, then again, is more savvy for huge shipments however includes longer travel times. Street and rail transportation might be reasonable for local exchange, giving adaptability and cost proficiency.

In the domain of worldwide exchange, the idea of Incoterms (Global Business Terms) assumes a significant part in characterizing the obligations and dangers among purchasers and venders. Incoterms indicate who is answerable for transportation expenses, protection, and customs leeway at each phase of the inventory network. Clear getting it and adherence to Incoterms assist with moderating errors, keep away from questions, and guarantee a smooth progression of products across borders.

Customs consistence is a key part of global production network the board. Various nations have shifting guidelines and necessities connected with import and commodity processes. Guaranteeing consistence with customs guidelines is imperative to forestalling postponements, fines, and disturbances in the production network. Organizations should explore complex documentation, levies, and import/send out limitations, requiring careful meticulousness and a proactive way to deal with consistence.

Risk the board is an inborn piece of worldwide exchange because of the different scope of difficulties and vulnerabilities. Cash variances, international pressures, catastrophic events, and worldwide wellbeing emergencies, as exemplified by the Coronavirus pandemic, can upset supply chains. Associations should direct exhaustive gamble appraisals, foster emergency courses of action, and lay out strong production network organizations to moderate the effect of unexpected occasions. Broadening providers, double obtaining basic parts, and keeping up with security stock are systems that improve production network strength notwithstanding worldwide vulnerabilities.

Social contemplations and correspondence challenges are predominant in global exchange and production network the board. Understanding the social subtleties of

EXPORT STRATEGIES

exchanging accomplices is fundamental for building viable connections and exploring strategic approaches. Language contrasts, time region abberations, and fluctuating correspondence styles can present difficulties. Stressing diverse preparation for production network experts and using correspondence advancements can assist with crossing over social holes and encourage cooperation.

Innovation assumes a critical part in upgrading global stock chains. The coordination of advanced arrangements, for example, blockchain, Web of Things (IoT), and computerized reasoning (man-made intelligence), improves perceivability, straightforwardness, and proficiency. Blockchain innovation, for example, gives a safe and carefully designed record for recording exchanges and following the progression of merchandise across the store network. IoT gadgets empower ongoing observing of shipments, guaranteeing perceivability into the area and state of items during travel. Artificial intelligence controlled investigation offer experiences into request estimating, stock improvement, and hazard the executives.

Joint effort and association building are fundamental parts of proficient worldwide production network the board. Laying areas of strength for out with providers, merchants, coordinated operations suppliers, and customs specialists encourages a consistent progression of data and products. Cooperative drives, for example, seller oversaw stock (VMI) and cooperative preparation, guaging, and recharging (CPFR), empower nearer coordination between exchanging accomplices, prompting further developed responsiveness and effectiveness in the production network.

Web based business has turned into a main impetus in global exchange, reshaping the scene of production network the executives. The development of online retail has prompted expanded interest for effective last-mile conveyance, assisted delivery, and smoothed out brings processes back. Associations should adjust their store network techniques to oblige the one of a kind necessities of internet business, including the requirement for vigorous request satisfaction frameworks, continuous stock perceivability, and client cordial bring processes back.

Manageability is an undeniably critical thought in worldwide store network the executives. As natural worries gain unmistakable quality, organizations are feeling the squeeze to embrace eco-accommodating practices all through their stock chains. This incorporates choosing economical materials, decreasing fossil fuel byproducts in transportation, and carrying out harmless to the ecosystem bundling arrangements. Maintainability lines up with corporate social obligation drives as well as satisfies the developing customer need for eco-cognizant items and mindful inventory network rehearses.

Key production network configuration is a basic part of global exchange, including choices connected with the design and setup of the inventory network organization. Factors like the number and area of creation offices, stockrooms, and dissemination focuses influence the productivity and responsiveness of the inventory network. Associations should cautiously consider the compromises among brought together and decentralized production network models, considering cost, lead time, and market necessities.

Worldwide production network perceivability is a foundation of successful global exchange. The capacity to track and screen the development of merchandise progressively gives associations significant bits of knowledge into the situation with shipments and likely issues. High level perceivability arrangements influence innovation, like RFID (Radio-Recurrence Distinguishing proof) and GPS (Worldwide Situating Framework), to improve ongoing following capacities. Further developed perceivability empowers proactive navigation, permitting associations to address interruptions expeditiously and streamline the progression of products across borders.

Administrative changes and economic deals altogether influence worldwide production network elements. Organizations should keep up to date with developing exchange arrangements, taxes, and economic accords that can impact the expense and possibility of global exchange. Changes in political scenes and the discussion of new economic agreements can present vulnerabilities, expecting associations to adjust their production network techniques appropriately.

All in all, productive store network the board in global exchange is a complex test that requires a key and all encompassing methodology. Associations should explore a complicated scene of operations, guidelines, social contrasts, and mechanical headways to guarantee the consistent progression of merchandise across borders. By utilizing cutting edge innovations, encouraging cooperation, and embracing supportable practices, organizations can upgrade the strength and productivity of their global stock chains. In a time of expanding globalization and interconnected economies, compelling worldwide production network the executives isn't just an upper hand however an essential for supported outcome in the worldwide commercial center.

7.2 Transportation modes and logistics considerations

Transportation modes and coordinated factors contemplations are major parts of production network the board, assuming a urgent part in the development of merchandise from the starting place to the last objective. The choice of transportation modes and the essential thought of operations processes have huge ramifications for cost, proficiency, and by and large inventory network execution. In this far reaching investigation, we dig into the different transportation modes and the basic planned operations contemplations that associations should explore to advance their stockpile chains.

Transportation Modes:
Street Transportation:
Street transportation is a flexible and broadly involved mode for the development of merchandise. It incorporates trucks, vans, and different vehicles that work on streets. Street transport offers adaptability, taking into consideration house to house conveyance, making it reasonable for both short-pull and long stretch shipments. The proficiency of street transportation is impacted by variables, for example, street

foundation, traffic conditions, and fuel costs. Be that as it may, it faces difficulties connected with blockage, administrative consistence, and ecological effect.

Rail Transportation:

Rail transportation is a productive mode for significant distance cargo development, especially for mass merchandise. Trains can convey huge volumes of freight overstretched distances, making rail a financially reasonable choice for specific ventures. Rail transportation is known for its eco-friendliness and diminished carbon impression contrasted with street transport. Notwithstanding, it is less adaptable concerning conveyance areas and may require extra truck transportation for the last mile.

Air Transportation:

Air transportation is the quickest mode for the development of merchandise, making it reasonable for time-touchy and high-esteem shipments. Airship cargo is ordinarily utilized for transitory merchandise, gadgets, and items with short timeframes of realistic usability. While air transport offers speed, it accompanies greater expenses contrasted with different modes. Freight space is restricted, and there are contemplations for security, customs methods, and the potential for flight delays.

Ocean Transportation:

Ocean transportation is a practical mode for the development of huge volumes of merchandise over significant distances. Compartment ships are generally utilized for worldwide exchange, giving a normalized and effective method for moving merchandise in holders. Ocean transportation is vital for enterprises like assembling, retail, and auto, where economies of scale and lower transportation costs are critical benefits. In any case, ocean transport includes longer travel times, presenting difficulties for time-touchy shipments.

Pipeline Transportation:

Pipeline transportation is a specific mode for the development of fluids and gases, like oil and flammable gas. Pipelines are effective for constant and mass transportation, especially in the energy area. While pipeline transport offers a consistent stream and limits natural effect, it requires critical forthright interest in framework and is restricted to explicit kinds of freight.

Planned operations Contemplations:

Store network Perceivability:

Store network perceivability is a basic coordinated factors thought that includes following and checking the development of merchandise at each stage. Trend setting innovations, including GPS following, RFID, and continuous checking frameworks, empower associations to acquire perceivability into their stockpile chains. Upgraded perceivability takes into account proactive navigation, convenient reactions to disturbances, and generally speaking better command over the production network.

Stock Administration:

Compelling stock administration is fundamental for keeping up with ideal stock levels and satisfying client need. Associations should work out some kind of harmony between holding sufficient stock to satisfy need and limiting conveying costs. In the nick of time (JIT) stock frameworks expect to decrease holding costs by guaranteeing that merchandise show up exactly when required in the creation cycle. Nonetheless, JIT frameworks require careful coordination and may practically rule out mistake.

Warehousing and Dispersion:

Warehousing and circulation are essential parts of operations, zeroing in on the effective stockpiling and treatment of stock. The essential position of stockrooms can altogether affect dispersion proficiency. Current stockrooms consolidate robotization and advanced mechanics to smooth out processes, decrease blunders, and upgrade by and large functional effectiveness. Effective warehousing guarantees that items are promptly accessible for request satisfaction while limiting stockpiling costs.

Last-Mile Conveyance:

Last-mile conveyance is the last leg of the store network, including the development of merchandise from a dispersion place to the end customer. It is a basic strategies thought, especially with regards to online business. Associations should improve last-mile conveyance to meet client assumptions for quick and solid help. The difficulties incorporate dealing with the intricacy of metropolitan conveyances, lessening conveyance times, and limiting the ecological effect of various little conveyances.

Turn around Planned operations:

Turn around planned operations includes overseeing item returns and reusing. As client assumptions for issue free return processes increment, associations should foster effective opposite planned operations techniques to limit costs and natural effect. This incorporates carrying out compelling merchandise exchanges, reusing programs, and renovating drives. Turn around strategies is pivotal for keeping up with consumer loyalty and streamlining the utilization of assets.

Administrative Consistence:

Administrative consistence is a huge coordinated operations thought, especially in worldwide exchange. Associations should explore a mind boggling trap of guidelines connected with customs, exchange, and transportation. Resistance can bring about postponements, fines, and reputational harm. Keeping up to date with administrative necessities and guaranteeing adherence is significant for the smooth progression of products across borders.

Innovation Coordination:

The coordination of innovation is a critical driver for streamlining operations processes. Trend setting innovations like Web of Things (IoT), man-made consciousness (artificial intelligence), and blockchain add to upgraded effectiveness and straightforwardness. IoT gadgets give continuous information on the area and state of products during travel. Artificial intelligence fueled investigation assist associations with examining information for request determining, stock improvement, and chance administration. Blockchain innovation guarantees secure and sealed exchanges, especially in complex stockpile chains.

Coordinated effort and Correspondence:

Coordinated effort and correspondence are fundamental components of successful operations. In a universally scattered production network, coordination between different partners, including providers, makers, wholesalers, and retailers, is vital. Correspondence innovations and coordinated effort stages work with continuous data sharing, empowering a more responsive and deft inventory network. Cooperative endeavors, for example, seller oversaw stock (VMI) and cooperative preparation, anticipating, and renewal (CPFR), improve coordination between exchanging accomplices.

Manageability Practices:

Manageability has turned into a focal concentration in strategies and store network the executives. Associations are under expanding strain to embrace eco-accommodating practices all through their stockpile chains. This incorporates supportable obtaining, lessening fossil fuel byproducts in transportation, and executing harmless to the ecosystem bundling arrangements. Manageability rehearses line up with corporate social obligation drives as well as fulfill the developing shopper need for eco-cognizant items and mindful inventory network rehearses.

Risk The executives:

Risk the board is an indispensable piece of strategies and store network the executives. Associations should recognize and evaluate likely dangers, foster alternate courses of action, and lay out tough store network organizations. This incorporates assessing the monetary strength of providers, surveying international dangers, and taking into account the effect of cataclysmic events or other unanticipated occasions. Compelling gamble the executives upgrades the capacity to answer interruptions instantly and guarantees the progression of production network activities.

Key Production network Plan:

Key production network configuration includes deciding the ideal design of the inventory network organization. This incorporates choices in regards to the number and area of offices, transportation courses, and stock arrangement. A very much planned production network considers factors, for example, cost, administration levels, and adaptability, expecting to accomplish an equilibrium that meets both client and hierarchical targets. Vital plan is significant for adjusting to changing economic situations and client necessities.

Globalization and Economic deals:

The globalization of supply chains enjoys the two benefits and difficulties. While it opens up new business sectors and permits organizations to source data sources and parts from various areas, it additionally acquaints intricacies related with international dangers, exchange questions, and shifting administrative conditions. Associations should remain informed about economic deals, duties, and international advancements that can affect the expense and possibility of global exchange.

Taking everything into account, transportation modes and operations contemplations are complicatedly connected to the productivity and viability of inventory network the board. The essential determination of transportation modes, combined with fastidious thoughtfulness regarding coordinated operations processes, is fundamental for associations looking to improve their stock chains, decrease expenses, and fulfill the developing needs of clients in a unique worldwide commercial center. As innovation proceeds to progress and the intricacies of global exchange persevere, remaining in front of operations patterns and embracing imaginative arrangements will be critical to keeping an upper hand in the consistently changing scene of store network the board.

7.3 Warehouse management and inventory control for global operations

Stockroom the board and stock control are basic parts of store network the executives, assuming an essential part in guaranteeing the effective progression of merchandise from creation to conveyance, and at last to the end shopper. With regards to worldwide tasks, where supply chains frequently range across landmasses and include different business sectors, powerful stockroom the executives and stock control become significantly really testing and essential. This investigation digs into the complexities of distribution center administration and stock control, looking at the key contemplations, difficulties, and techniques that associations utilize to improve these parts of their worldwide inventory chains.

Stockroom The executives:

Key Distribution center Area:

The essential situation of distribution centers is a key thought in worldwide tasks. Stockroom areas influence transportation costs, lead times, and in general conveyance effectiveness. Associations should evaluate factors like closeness to providers and clients, transportation foundation, and administrative contemplations while deciding distribution center areas.

The objective is to lay out an organization of decisively found stockrooms that limits transportation costs while guaranteeing opportune and financially savvy conveyance to end buyers.

Stockroom Plan and Design:

The plan and design of stockrooms altogether impact functional effectiveness. Present day distribution centers influence cutting edge innovations, mechanization, and wise plan standards to advance space use and smooth out processes. Productive stockroom configuration incorporates contemplations for capacity frameworks, picking ways, and material taking care of hardware. Computerization advancements, like mechanical frameworks and robotized directed vehicles (AGVs), upgrade speed and precision in stockroom activities.

Stock Opening:

Stock opening includes decisively setting items inside the distribution center to enhance picking and pressing cycles. Quick things are regularly positioned nearer to delivery regions for faster access, while more slow moving things might be put away in less available areas. The objective is to limit travel time for stockroom laborers and further develop by and large request satisfaction proficiency. Stock opening is a continuous cycle that requires ordinary audit and change in view of item request designs.

Innovation Joining in Stockroom The executives Frameworks (WMS):

Stockroom The executives Frameworks (WMS) are vital to current distribution center activities. These frameworks influence innovation to give ongoing perceivability into stock, computerize cycles, and improve generally speaking effectiveness. WMS arrangements coordinate with other store network innovations, for example, Venture Asset Arranging (ERP) frameworks and transportation the executives frameworks, making a consistent progression of data across the store network. Scanner tag examining, RFID innovation, and voice picking frameworks are instances of advances normally incorporated into WMS for further developed precision and speed.

Cross-Mooring and Parcel:

Cross-mooring and parcel are techniques utilized to limit distribution center capacity and taking care of. Cross-docking includes moving products straightforwardly from inbound to outbound transportation with practically zero in the middle between. Parcel includes moving products starting with one transportation vehicle then onto the next without middle warehousing. These methodologies are especially applicable in worldwide tasks where limiting stock holding expenses and accelerating the progression of products are fundamental contemplations.

Request Satisfaction Techniques:

Request satisfaction techniques include the cycles from getting client orders to transportation items. Associations should adjust the speed of request satisfaction with cost contemplations. Systems might incorporate cluster picking, wave picking, or zone picking, contingent upon variables like request volume, item attributes, and client assumptions.

The execution of innovation, like request the board frameworks and computerized picking arrangements, adds to more productive and exact request satisfaction.

Stock Control:

Request Determining and Arranging:

Exact interest guaging is an essential component of successful stock control. Associations should investigate authentic deals information, market patterns, and outer variables to figure interest for their items. High level guaging strategies, including AI calculations, improve the precision of interest forecasts. A vigorous interest arranging process guarantees that associations keep up with the right degree of stock to satisfy client need while abstaining from overloading or stockouts.

Security Stock Administration:

Wellbeing stock is a cradle stock held to moderate the gamble of stockouts because of unforeseen changes popular or store network interruptions. Deciding the fitting degree of security stock includes considering elements, for example, request fluctuation, lead times, and provider unwavering quality. Associations should figure out some kind of harmony between guaranteeing item accessibility and limiting the conveying costs related with abundance stock. Ceaseless checking and change of well-being stock levels are pivotal for dynamic inventory chains.

ABC Examination:

ABC examination arranges stock into three gatherings in view of their significance and worth. "A" things are high-esteem, basic items that normally address a more modest part of in general stock. "B" things are tolerably significant, and "C" things are lower-esteem things that make up most of stock. This arrangement assists associations with focusing on stock administration endeavors. For instance, "A" things might require more successive checking and more tight control to forestall stockouts.

Cycle Counting and Stock Reviews:

Ordinary cycle counting and stock reviews are fundamental for keeping up with exact stock records. Cycle counting includes counting a subset of stock things on a planned premise, turning through various things over the long haul. This approach limits interruption to day to day activities and distinguishes errors among recorded and genuine stock levels. Intermittent full stock reviews give a thorough survey and compromise of all stock things.

Provider Coordinated effort and Merchant Oversaw Stock (VMI):

Cooperative associations with providers are critical for compelling stock control. Seller Oversaw Stock (VMI) is a cooperative game plan where the provider deals with the stock levels at the client's distribution center. Through ongoing information sharing, providers can screen stock levels and recharge stock depending on the situation. VMI decreases the weight on the client to oversee and conjecture stock, prompting further developed production network effectiveness.

Innovation in Stock Control:

Innovation assumes a focal part in stock control, giving devices to constant following, perceivability, and examination. Scanner tag checking, RFID innovation, and IoT gadgets empower exact following of stock developments. Stock control frameworks incorporated with ERP and WMS work with consistent information stream and navigation. Progressed examination and simulated intelligence controlled arrangements add to further developed request estimating and enhancement of stock levels.

Bunch and Part Following:

Bunch and part following is basic, particularly in businesses where items have explicit assembling or termination dates. This is normal in areas like drugs, food and drink, and gadgets. Following the development of bunches or parts guarantees discernibility all through the inventory network. In the event of reviews or quality issues, associations can quickly distinguish impacted items and make fitting remedial moves.

Financial Request Amount (EOQ) and Reorder Point:

Financial Request Amount (EOQ) is a recipe that works out the ideal request amount to limit all out stock expenses, including requesting expenses and holding costs. The reorder point is the stock level at which another request ought to be put to keep away from stockouts. These estimations are vital parts of stock control, assisting associations with deciding when and the amount to reorder to keep up with ideal stock levels while limiting expenses.

Serialization and Recognizability:
Serialization includes doling out an extraordinary identifier, like a chronic number or standardized tag, to individual units of an item. This works with detectability all through the store network, empowering associations to track and follow the development of items from creation to utilization. Serialization is especially significant in businesses where administrative consistence and item genuineness are foremost.

Difficulties and Techniques in Stockroom The board and Stock Control for Worldwide Tasks:

Production network Intricacy:
Worldwide stock chains frequently include numerous providers, fabricating offices, and appropriation focuses across various nations. The intricacy of overseeing different tasks can prompt difficulties in keeping up with perceivability and command over stock. Associations address this intricacy by carrying out trend setting innovations for ongoing following, utilizing unified data frameworks, and cultivating cooperation with worldwide accomplices.

Lead Time Fluctuation:
Fluctuation in lead times, particularly in worldwide stockpile chains, can affect stock preparation. Longer lead times might require viewing more elevated levels of wellbeing stock to be answerable for possible postponements.
Associations moderate lead time changeability by working intimately with providers, utilizing innovation for continuous correspondence, and utilizing dynamic stock control systems that adjust to changing lead time situations.

Administrative Consistence:
Worldwide tasks expect adherence to different administrative systems connected with customs, import/send out guidelines, and industry-explicit norms. Consistence difficulties can bring about deferrals, fines, and interruptions. Associations stay consistent by remaining informed about administrative changes, carrying out strong documentation processes, and using innovation arrangements that mechanize consistence techniques.

Request Instability:
Worldwide business sectors are likely to request unpredictability affected by elements like financial circumstances, international occasions, and customer patterns. Associations address request instability through nimble store network techniques, responsive estimating models, and dynamic stock control systems. Cooperative associations with providers and clients add to quicker variation to changing interest designs.

Innovation Reconciliation Difficulties:

Coordinating assorted advancements across worldwide tasks can be trying because of similarity issues, contrasting guidelines, and fluctuating degrees of innovation reception among accomplices. Associations take on normalized innovation stages, influence cloud-based arrangements, and lay out clear correspondence conventions to address incorporation challenges. The utilization of Use Programming Connection points (APIs) works with consistent information trade between various frameworks.

Ecological and Manageability Contemplations:

Supportability contemplations are acquiring noticeable quality in distribution center administration and stock control. Associations center around eco-accommodating works on, including energy-productive stockroom plan, manageable bundling, and capable obtaining. Economical practices line up with corporate social obligation objectives as well as resound with naturally cognizant shoppers, adding to a positive brand picture.

Arising Advancements Affecting Distribution center Administration and Stock Control:

The reception of arising innovations essentially influences stockroom the board and stock control. Advanced mechanics and computerization innovations, like independent versatile robots (AMRs) and automated picking frameworks, upgrade productivity and lessen work costs. Man-made consciousness and AI add to cutting edge request anticipating and streamlining of stock levels. Blockchain innovation guarantees straightforwardness and detectability in the store network, addressing concerns connected with item credibility and duplicating.

Ability The executives and Preparing:

The compelling administration of stockroom activities requires gifted work force who comprehend the intricacies of worldwide stockpile chains and are capable in utilizing trend setting innovations. Associations put resources into ability advancement programs, give continuous preparation on new innovations, and focus on labor force the board to guarantee that faculty are prepared to deal with the difficulties of present day distribution center administration and stock control.

Stock control assumes a critical part in the effective administration of worldwide tasks. In a world described by interconnected supply chains and quick changes in market elements, successful stock administration turns into an essential basic for organizations meaning to remain serious. This unpredictable cycle includes regulating the obtaining, stockpiling, and dissemination of products in a way that lines up with hierarchical objectives and client requests. Fruitful stock control not just guarantees the accessibility of items when and where they are required yet additionally adds to cost decrease, smoothed out tasks, and further developed consumer loyalty.

One of the essential goals of stock control in worldwide tasks is to work out some kind of harmony among organic market. Keeping an ideal degree of stock is pivotal to forestall stockouts, overload circumstances, and related monetary repercussions. This fragile harmony is additionally convoluted by the difficulties of overseeing stock across various geological areas, managing shifting interest designs, and exploring through the intricacies of worldwide coordinated operations.

In the worldwide scene, organizations work in different business sectors with particular social, monetary, and administrative conditions. Subsequently, stock control techniques should be versatile and receptive to the special requests of every district. This requires a nuanced comprehension of nearby market patterns, shopper ways of behaving, and production network subtleties. Moreover, the impact of international variables, for example, exchange strategies and taxes, further highlights the significance of a hearty stock control system that can explore and moderate possible interruptions.

One vital part of worldwide stock control is request anticipating. Precise forecasts of future interest empower associations to adjust their stock levels as needs be, limiting the gamble of stockouts or abundance stock. Utilizing progressed determining models, information investigation, and man-made brainpower can upgrade the precision of expectations, considering different factors, for example, irregularity, market patterns, and monetary pointers.

In a worldwide setting, the strategies of stock administration reach out past public lines. Proficient transportation, customs freedom, and worldwide delivery assume basic parts in guaranteeing a consistent progression of products across borders. Joint effort with solid strategies accomplices and a perfectly tuned inventory network are fundamental parts of successful worldwide stock control.

Additionally, utilizing innovation arrangements, for example, following and perceivability apparatuses, can upgrade constant checking of stock developments, giving experiences into expected bottlenecks or postponements.

The reception of innovation is a foundation of current stock control frameworks. Computerized stock administration frameworks use standardized tag examining, RFID (Radio Recurrence Recognizable proof), and different advances to smooth out the following and observing of stock. These frameworks lessen the probability of mistakes as well as add to the effectiveness and speed of stock related processes. Mix with other endeavor frameworks, like ERP (Venture Asset Arranging) and CRM (Client Relationship The executives), guarantees a firm and synchronized way to deal with stock control inside the more extensive hierarchical system.

Moreover, the ascent of online business and omnichannel retail has added layers of intricacy to worldwide stock control. The interest for consistent client encounters across different channels expects organizations to keep up with precise, ongoing stock perceivability. Incorporated stock control frameworks that solidify information from different channels empower associations to oversee stock levels successfully, forestall stockouts, and advance satisfaction processes.

Vital seller the executives is one more basic part of worldwide stock control. Co-operative associations with providers, both neighborhood and worldwide, can add to further developed lead times, cost effectiveness, and generally inventory network versatility. Building solid associations includes powerful correspondence, straightforward data sharing, and common trust. Associations should likewise be skilled at overseeing provider connections in various districts, understanding and adjusting to social subtleties, administrative prerequisites, and market elements.

Risk the executives is a fundamental piece of worldwide stock control. Organizations face different dangers, including international vulnerabilities, cataclysmic events, store network disturbances, and variances in cash trade rates. A strong gamble the executives procedure includes situation arranging, broadening of providers, and the improvement of alternate courses of action to relieve expected disturbances. Also, the utilization of information examination and prescient displaying can assist with distinguishing likely dangers and empower proactive measures to limit their effect on stock administration.

The idea of in the nick of time (JIT) stock administration has acquired conspicuousness in worldwide tasks. JIT underlines limiting stock levels to decrease conveying costs while guaranteeing that items are accessible precisely when required. While JIT offers benefits, for example, cost reserve funds and further developed proficiency, it additionally requires exact coordination and synchronization across the whole store network. In the worldwide setting, the difficulties related with JIT execution incorporate longer lead times, transportation delays, and the requirement for hearty emergency courses of action.

Stock control is intently attached to monetary contemplations. Conveying costs, which incorporate capacity, protection, and out of date quality, can fundamentally influence the general productivity of a business. Associations should figure out some kind of harmony between keeping up with adequate stock to satisfy need and limiting conveying costs. Innovation driven arrangements that give perceivability into stock turnover, request designs, and conveying costs engage organizations to pursue informed choices that line up with their monetary targets.

In the domain of worldwide tasks, social knowledge assumes a critical part in stock control. Understanding and regarding the social subtleties of various areas impact correspondence styles, discussion approaches, and relationship-building methodologies. This social mindfulness stretches out to stock administration rehearses, where neighborhood customs, inclinations, and business standards might affect the decision of stock control methodologies and the general progress of worldwide tasks.

Powerful correspondence is fundamental in the coordination of stock control exercises across assorted areas. Worldwide partnerships frequently work with groups scattered universally, requiring consistent correspondence channels and normalized processes. Clear correspondence guarantees that everybody in the store network, from providers to wholesalers, is in total agreement with respect to stock levels, request gauges, and any possible difficulties.

Persistent improvement is a crucial standard in worldwide stock control. Consistently assessing and enhancing stock administration processes, utilizing innovation progressions, and integrating examples gained from previous encounters add to a light-footed and versatile stock control system. Associations should encourage a culture of development and be available to embracing new techniques and innovations that improve the productivity and viability of their stock control systems.

Chapter 8

Marketing and Promotion in International Markets

Showcasing and advancement in worldwide business sectors are significant parts of an organization's worldwide procedure. As organizations extend past their home-grown lines, they experience different societies, inclinations, and market elements. Really exploring these intricacies requires a smart and versatile way to deal with showcasing and advancement.

One of the critical difficulties in global showcasing is figuring out the social subtleties that shape shopper conduct. Social contrasts can altogether affect how items and messages are seen. Along these lines, fruitful worldwide showcasing systems should be socially delicate and customized to neighborhood inclinations. This requires exhaustive statistical surveying to acquire bits of knowledge into the interest group's qualities, convictions, and purchasing ways of behaving.

Language is one more basic consider worldwide promoting. Conveying successfully in the neighborhood language fabricates trust and compatibility with the main interest group. Interpreting content precisely isn't just about changing over words yet additionally about passing on the planned message and social setting. Brands should put resources into proficient interpretation administrations and restriction to guarantee that their advertising materials resound with the main interest group.

Notwithstanding etymological contemplations, adjusting limited time systems to the administrative climate of every nation is fundamental. Various nations have unmistakable lawful systems, promoting principles, and social responsive qualities. Understanding and following these guidelines is crucial to staying away from lawful issues and keeping a positive brand picture.

The globalization of business sectors has prompted the ascent of normalized showcasing systems, where organizations keep up with predictable marking and informing across various nations. Be that as it may, accomplishing a harmony among normalization and restriction is critical. While certain components can be normalized for effectiveness and brand consistency, others might should be custom fitted to explicit social settings to reverberate with nearby shoppers.

Web-based entertainment has turned into an incredible asset for global showcasing and advancement. Stages like Facebook, Instagram, and Twitter have a worldwide reach, empowering organizations to interface with different crowds. Notwithstanding, the viability of web-based entertainment crusades relies upon understanding the stage inclinations of each market and making content that lines up with neighborhood patterns and interests.

Diverse buyer conduct additionally impacts item situating and marking. An item that is situated as an extravagance thing in one market might be seen diversely in another. Organizations should adjust their marking systems to line up with the nearby impression of significant worth and quality. This requires a profound comprehension of social mentalities towards brands and utilization.

The decision of advertising channels is another basic thought. While advanced stations are common in many business sectors, customary types of promoting like TV, radio, print media actually hold importance in specific locales. A complete global promoting procedure ought to use a blend of channels to contact an expansive crowd.

Building solid associations with nearby powerhouses can be a successful method for acquiring validity and arrive at an interest group. Powerhouses who are very much respected in a particular market can assist with overcoming any barrier between a brand and its expected clients. Nonetheless, the determination of powerhouses ought to line up with the social qualities and inclinations of the objective market.

Besides, worldwide showcasing requires an essential way to deal with evaluating. Factors, for example, nearby buying power, rivalry, and saw esteem impact evaluating choices. Organizations should direct exhaustive market examination to decide ideal valuing techniques that augment benefit while staying cutthroat in each market.

Worldwide brands frequently face the test of adjusting a predictable brand picture with the requirement for neighborhood significance. This is especially significant in business sectors where purchasers put a high worth on realness and nearby character. Fruitful worldwide brands track down ways of coordinating nearby components into their showcasing systems without compromising the general brand character.

The advanced time has achieved huge changes in buyer conduct, with web based shopping turning out to be progressively predominant around the world. Web based business has opened new open doors for organizations to arrive at worldwide clients without the requirement for actual presence in each market. Nonetheless, exploring the intricacies of cross-line internet business, including strategies, installment frameworks, and lawful contemplations, requires cautious preparation.

Information examination assumes a urgent part in upgrading worldwide promoting endeavors. Breaking down customer conduct, crusade execution, and market patterns gives important bits of knowledge that empower organizations to refine their procedures. Utilizing information driven direction permits organizations to adjust rapidly to changing economic situations and purchaser inclinations.

In worldwide business sectors, contest can be wild, and separation is critical. Organizations should recognize their one of a kind incentives and convey them successfully to hang out in jam-packed markets. This requires a profound comprehension of the serious scene and an essential way to deal with situating the brand in the personalities of shoppers.

Emergency the board is an essential part of global showcasing. Worldwide organizations face the gamble of political, financial, and social difficulties that can affect their tasks. Having alternate courses of action set up and being ready to adjust procedures because of unexpected occasions is fundamental for relieving gambles and guaranteeing business progression.

The job of government and administrative bodies can't be neglected in global promoting. Exchange strategies, levies, and discretionary relations can influence the simplicity of carrying on with work in a specific country. Organizations should remain informed about international turns of events and draw in with nearby specialists to actually explore administrative difficulties.

Organizations and joint efforts with neighborhood organizations can be instrumental in laying out areas of strength for an in global business sectors. Nearby accomplices bring important bits of knowledge, connections, and social comprehension that can improve the viability of advertising techniques. Framing key coalitions likewise mitigates the dangers related with entering new business sectors.

Client criticism and surveys assume a huge part in forming brand discernment in worldwide business sectors. Online stages give a space to clients to impart their encounters and insights. Effectively checking and answering client criticism exhibits a guarantee to consumer loyalty and can emphatically influence brand notoriety.

Supportability and corporate social obligation (CSR) have become progressively significant contemplations for worldwide shoppers. Organizations that focus on moral strategic approaches and add to social and natural causes reverberate with cognizant purchasers. Incorporating manageability into showcasing messages can upgrade brand picture and draw in a socially capable client base.

All in all, showcasing and advancement in worldwide business sectors require a comprehensive and versatile methodology. Social responsiveness, semantic contemplations, administrative consistence, and a profound comprehension of neighborhood customer conduct are fundamental components of fruitful global showcasing methodologies.

Utilizing computerized channels, information examination, and key organizations improves the viability of promoting endeavors in a globalized world. As organizations explore the intricacies of worldwide business sectors, they should stay nimble, receptive to change, and focused on areas of strength for building with different crowds.

8.1 Crafting a global marketing strategy

Making a worldwide promoting system is a multi-layered try that includes cautious preparation, statistical surveying, and a comprehension of the intricacies innate in contacting different crowds across the globe. In an interconnected world, organizations looking to extend universally should foster an essential methodology that rises above geological limits and adjusts to the subtleties of various business sectors.

The underpinning of a fruitful worldwide promoting technique lies in exhaustive statistical surveying. Understanding the social, financial, and social elements of target markets is fundamental for fitting showcasing endeavors to resound with nearby buyers. This includes digging into shopper conduct, inclinations, and patterns extraordinary to every area, as well as acquiring experiences into the cutthroat scene.

Restriction is a vital part of creating a worldwide promoting methodology. While there might be a compulsion to apply a one-size-fits-all methodology, fruitful worldwide brands perceive the significance of adjusting their informing to suit the social setting of each market. This incorporates language interpretation, social responsiveness, and a familiarity with nearby standards and values. Brands that can consistently coordinate with neighborhood societies are bound to lay out a significant association with purchasers.

Language assumes a urgent part in successful correspondence. Deciphering advertising materials precisely is critical, yet it goes past simple language transformation. It includes figuring out the social subtleties, phrases, and setting to guarantee that the message resounds with the target group. Putting resources into proficient interpretation administrations and social experts is a reasonable move toward accomplishing this degree of precision.

The computerized age has changed the scene of worldwide promoting, offering organizations phenomenal chances to contact global crowds through internet based channels. Web-based entertainment stages, web search tools, and online business entrances give a worldwide stage for brands to grandstand their items and draw in with different shopper bases. Making a computerized showcasing system that use these stages is principal for worldwide achievement.

Virtual entertainment, specifically, has turned into an integral asset for global promoting. Stages like Facebook, Instagram, and Twitter rise above borders, empowering brands to interface with buyers around the world. Nonetheless, it's urgent to comprehend the stage inclinations in various areas and designer content in like manner. Social importance and awareness in online entertainment crusades add to building valid associations with crowds.

Online business has arisen as a distinct advantage in worldwide business, permitting organizations to arrive at buyers in far off business sectors without the requirement for actual retail facades. Nonetheless, the difficulties of cross-line web based business ought to be acknowledged with a sober mind. Organizations should address strategic intricacies, explore assorted installment frameworks, and stick to lawful contemplations intended for each market.

Finding some kind of harmony among normalization and confinement is a ceaseless test in worldwide showcasing. While consistency in marking encourages a durable worldwide personality, there is a need to adjust specific components to line up with neighborhood inclinations. Normalizing center brand components while considering adaptability in informing and special exercises is a fragile yet important balance.

Worldwide advertising techniques ought to be discerning of the estimating elements in various business sectors. Factors, for example, nearby buying power, rivalry, and saw esteem all impact evaluating choices. A nuanced comprehension of these elements permits organizations to carry out evaluating systems that expand productivity while staying serious and interesting to neighborhood purchasers.

Besides, the decision of promoting diverts is urgent in a worldwide system. While advanced stations are unavoidable, customary types of promoting like TV, radio, print actually hold importance in specific districts. Making an extensive technique that consolidates a blend of channels guarantees that brands contact a different crowd with changing media utilization propensities.

Powerhouse showcasing has turned into a pervasive procedure in many business sectors, utilizing the compass and believability of neighborhood forces to be reckoned with to associate with interest groups. Distinguishing powerhouses who line up with the brand and are very much respected in unambiguous business sectors can give an important lift to worldwide showcasing endeavors. Nonetheless, cautious thought should be given to social fit and legitimacy.

Item situating and marking are complicatedly attached to social insights. What might be viewed as a top notch item in one market could be seen diversely in another. Creating a predictable yet versatile marking methodology that lines up with neighborhood impression of significant worth and quality is basic for worldwide achievement.

Worldwide brands should likewise wrestle with the test of keeping up with genuineness in assorted markets. Customers in various areas frequently esteem credibility and might have one or two misgivings of brands that show up excessively normalized or detached from neighborhood real factors. Effective worldwide brands track down ways of coordinating neighborhood components into their advertising methodologies without weakening the general brand personality.

Information investigation is a foundation of a powerful worldwide showcasing procedure. Examining shopper conduct, crusade execution, and market patterns gives noteworthy bits of knowledge that empower organizations to persistently refine their systems. Bridling the force of information driven independent direction permits organizations to adjust rapidly to changing economic situations and buyer inclinations.

Exploring the complexities of global business sectors requires a sharp familiarity with international elements and administrative scenes. Government approaches, economic accords, and lawful structures change starting with one country then onto the next, affecting the simplicity of carrying on with work. Organizations should keep up to date with these turns of events and proactively draw in with neighborhood specialists to guarantee consistence and explore expected difficulties.

Organizations and coordinated efforts with neighborhood organizations can be instrumental in laying out areas of strength for an in worldwide business sectors. Nearby accomplices bring significant bits of knowledge, laid out networks, and a nuanced comprehension of the market. Shaping key collusions works with market section as well as improves the validity and acknowledgment of the brand in new domains.

Supportability and corporate social obligation (CSR) have become progressively significant contemplations for worldwide purchasers. Organizations that focus on moral strategic policies and add to social and natural causes can construct a positive brand picture. Coordinating manageability into promoting messages reverberates with socially cognizant buyers and can be a differentiator in serious business sectors.

Emergency the board is a basic part of any worldwide showcasing procedure. Organizations working in numerous nations face the gamble of political, financial, and social difficulties that can affect their activities. Having hearty emergency courses of action set up, alongside the adaptability to adjust systems in light of unexpected occasions, is fundamental for relieving chances and guaranteeing business coherence.

Client criticism and online surveys employ huge impact in forming brand discernment worldwide. The period of advanced availability permits customers to generally impart their encounters and insights. Effectively observing and answering client criticism exhibits a guarantee to consumer loyalty as well as gives a valuable chance to address concerns and construct trust.

All in all, creating a worldwide promoting procedure requires a comprehensive and versatile methodology. Careful statistical surveying, social awareness, and restriction are principal to fitting promoting endeavors to different crowds. Utilizing advanced channels, figuring out the subtleties of evaluating and marking, and embracing information driven navigation add to the viability of worldwide promoting drives.

Exploring administrative scenes, shaping vital associations, and focusing on manageability are necessary components of progress in the mind boggling and interconnected universe of global business. By embracing these standards, organizations can situate themselves for maintainable development and accomplishment on the worldwide stage.

8.2 Leveraging digital marketing for international reach

Utilizing advanced showcasing for worldwide reach is a basic for organizations looking to grow their worldwide impression in the interconnected universe of the 21st 100 years. The computerized scene furnishes extraordinary chances to interface with different crowds, rise above geological limits, and fabricate brand mindfulness on a worldwide scale. In any case, exploring the intricacies of global computerized showcasing requires an essential methodology that thinks about social subtleties, language varieties, and the assorted inclinations of shoppers across various business sectors.

At the center of a fruitful global computerized showcasing methodology is the acknowledgment that a one-size-fits-all approach is lacking. Each market has its special attributes, and understanding these subtleties is basic for fitting computerized crusades successfully. Social responsiveness assumes a urgent part, impacting all that from content creation to the timing and tone of correspondence.

Language, as a vital part of culture, is a basic thought in worldwide computerized promoting. While English is generally spoken and perceived, it isn't the essential language for a huge piece of the worldwide populace. Putting resources into exact language interpretation and restriction of content is fundamental for guaranteeing that promoting messages resound with the interest group in their local language and social setting.

Website improvement (Search engine optimization) is a key part in the computerized showcasing weapons store, and its significance enhances with regards to global reach. Understanding the catchphrases and search terms applicable to each market is significant for improving substance and guaranteeing perceivability in neighborhood web crawler results. A nuanced way to deal with Website optimization, taking into account provincial varieties in language and search conduct, upgrades the viability of computerized promoting endeavors.

Web-based entertainment stages are useful assets for worldwide reach, giving a worldwide stage to brands to draw in with crowds continuously. Every area has its favored virtual entertainment channels, and understanding these inclinations is imperative for making designated crusades. Additionally, adjusting content to line up with social patterns and awarenesses is vital to cultivating significant associations on friendly stages.

The ascent of powerhouse showcasing has reshaped the advanced scene, offering brands a road to interface with crowds through confided in figures.

Utilizing neighborhood powerhouses who reverberate with the objective market can enhance the compass and effect of computerized crusades. Notwithstanding, cautious thought should be given to social fit and realness to guarantee that powerhouse organizations line up with the brand message.

Content promoting stays a foundation of computerized techniques for global reach. Making convincing and pertinent substance that addresses the qualities and interests of the interest group is fundamental. This goes past interpretation; it requires a profound comprehension of social subtleties to properly tailor content. Video content, specifically, has acquired conspicuousness worldwide, giving a visual and connecting method for imparting messages.

Email promoting, when executed in a calculated way, can be a strong device for global commitment. Building sectioned email records in light of local inclinations and conveying designated content improves the importance of email crusades. Be that as it may, regarding security guidelines and complying to global email promoting regulations is essential to stay away from legitimate traps.

Web based business has changed the manner in which organizations work universally, offering a road for organizations to arrive at shoppers in far off business sectors without the requirement for actual retail facades. A powerful global web based business methodology includes tending to strategic difficulties, giving a consistent internet shopping experience, and offering limited installment choices. Security and information protection contemplations are central to fabricate trust among global clients.

Information examination is a key part in the time of computerized showcasing, giving bits of knowledge that illuminate key navigation. Dissecting client conduct, commitment measurements, and transformation rates permits organizations to persistently upgrade crusades. In the global setting, information examination turns out to be considerably more basic, assisting organizations with figuring out the exhibition of missions in various business sectors and adjust systems likewise.

Personalization is a vital pattern in computerized promoting, and it turns out to be particularly pertinent with regards to worldwide reach. Fitting substance and informing in view of client inclinations, ways of behaving, and social elements improves the client experience and cultivates a feeling of association with the brand. Limitation goes past language; it includes grasping the social subtleties that shape shopper insights.

Portable showcasing is progressively significant in a worldwide setting, especially in districts where cell phones are the essential method for getting to the web. Upgrading sites, messages, and commercials for versatile stages guarantees that brands actually arrive at purchasers across different business sectors. Portable applications, if pertinent to the ideal interest group, can likewise be an important resource in global promoting.

Video conferencing and online classes have become essential parts of computerized correspondence, particularly directly following worldwide occasions that have sped up the reception of remote work and virtual connections. Utilizing these devices for worldwide advertising permits organizations to associate straightforwardly with crowds, direct virtual occasions, and grandstand items or administrations progressively.

Vital organizations with neighborhood organizations and computerized stages can altogether improve the viability of worldwide advanced showcasing endeavors. Neighborhood accomplices bring experiences into market elements, social subtleties, and buyer ways of behaving, empowering organizations to really explore new regions more. Coordinated efforts with web based business stages, online entertainment powerhouses, or neighborhood content makers can give admittance to laid out crowds.

Emergency the executives in the computerized domain requires a proactive methodology. Worldwide organizations should be ready to address likely emergencies, whether they be connected with item issues, advertising difficulties, or unanticipated worldwide occasions. Having an emergency correspondence plan set up, which incorporates a system for computerized channels, assists organizations with answering quickly and successfully to relieve reputational harm.

Administrative consistence is a basic thought in worldwide computerized promoting. Security regulations, information insurance guidelines, and promoting norms fluctuate starting with one country then onto the next. Organizations should keep up to date with these guidelines and guarantee that their computerized promoting rehearses line up with neighborhood legitimate prerequisites to stay away from punishments and keep a positive brand picture.

Worldwide network safety concerns feature the significance of getting advanced resources and client information. Worldwide organizations are powerless to digital dangers, and a break can have broad outcomes. Executing powerful network safety measures, including encryption, secure installment passages, and normal reviews, is basic to safeguard both the business and its clients in the computerized domain.

Manageability and corporate social obligation (CSR) have become compelling variables in purchaser direction. Organizations with a solid obligation to moral practices and social or ecological causes can use computerized stages to impart their qualities. Coordinating maintainability into computerized showcasing messages reverberates with socially cognizant purchasers and adds to building a positive brand picture.

All in all, utilizing computerized showcasing for global arrive at requests an extensive and nuanced approach. Social awareness, language restriction, and a comprehension of territorial inclinations are fundamental for fitting computerized crusades really.

The essential utilization of Website optimization, virtual entertainment, powerhouse showcasing, content creation, and online business augments the effect of computerized endeavors in different business sectors. Information investigation, personalization, and an emphasis on portable stages upgrade the client experience and drive commitment. Vital organizations, emergency the board arranging, administrative consistence, and network safety measures are indispensable components of a strong worldwide computerized promoting technique. By embracing these contemplations, organizations can explore the intricacies of the worldwide computerized scene and position themselves for progress on the global stage.

8.3 Cultural considerations in advertising and promotion

Social contemplations in publicizing and advancement are of central significance in the dynamic and various scene of worldwide business. As organizations extend universally, they experience a heap of social subtleties that essentially impact buyer conduct, insights, and buying choices. Making publicizing and limited time techniques that resound with the social sensibilities of different crowds is fundamental for building brand liking, laying out validity, and driving fruitful missions across borders.

Social responsiveness starts with an inside and out comprehension of the main interest group's qualities, convictions, and accepted practices. Various societies have unmistakable approaches to deciphering images, varieties, and messages. What might be seen as certain in one culture could be seen contrastingly in another. For example, red might represent karma in Chinese culture however mean peril in Western societies. Sponsors should put time and assets in social exploration to keep away from coincidental stumbles that could distance expected clients.

Language is an essential transporter of culture, and phonetic contemplations assume a urgent part in powerful correspondence. Past simple interpretation, publicists should guarantee that their messages are socially important and nuanced in the neighborhood language. Colloquial articulations, humor, and word decisions can fluctuate fundamentally, and strict interpretations may not catch the expected importance. Working with proficient interpreters who comprehend the social setting is fundamental to precisely pass on messages.

Social contrasts likewise manifest in correspondence styles. A few societies esteem immediate and unequivocal correspondence, while others lean toward more circuitous and nuanced informing. Sponsors need to adjust their tone and style to line up with the correspondence inclinations of the ideal interest group. Understanding the social subtleties of high-setting and low-setting correspondence societies is significant for creating publicizing messages that resound successfully.

The depiction of orientation jobs and generalizations changes broadly across societies. Promoters should be receptive to social perspectives towards orientation to guarantee that their missions are deferential and comprehensive. In certain societies, customary orientation jobs might be profoundly imbued, while others might be more moderate.

Finding some kind of harmony that regards social standards while testing destructive generalizations requires cautious thought and social knowledge.

Visual symbolism holds critical social weight and can pass on messages more effectively than words alone. The utilization of images, symbols, and visual illustrations ought to line up with the social setting to stay away from error. Also, various portrayal in visual substance is significant for inclusivity. Publicists ought to endeavor to portray a scope of identities, societies, and ways of life to resound with the different foundations of their crowd.

Understanding the social idea of time is essential in publicizing and advancement. A few societies put a high worth on dependability and proficiency, while others focus on a more loose and adaptable way to deal with time. Sponsors should be aware of social mentalities towards time to guarantee that their missions line up with nearby assumptions and don't coincidentally convey an absence of understanding.

Strict convictions and practices are profoundly imbued in many societies and can fundamentally affect purchaser conduct. Sponsors should explore strict responsive qualities with care, keeping away from content that could be seen as impolite or hostile. Fitting efforts to line up with strict schedules, occasions, and customs can show social mindfulness and cultivate a positive association with the crowd.

Humor, frequently an integral asset in publicizing, is exceptionally culture-subordinate. What might be silly in one culture could crash and burn or even affront in another. Sponsors need to painstakingly choose and make humor that reverberates with the social sensibilities of their main interest group. Nearby joke artists or humor advisors with social skill can be significant resources in such manner.

Social contemplations stretch out past the substance of publicizing to the selection of media channels. Various societies have differing media utilization propensities, with inclinations for TV, radio, print, or computerized stages. Sponsors should tailor their media procedures to line up with nearby inclinations to guarantee greatest reach and effect. Also, understanding the administrative climate for promoting in every nation is significant to follow nearby principles.

Social allotment is a delicate issue that publicists should explore with alert. Getting components from a culture without understanding or regarding their importance can prompt kickback and harm brand notoriety. Sponsors ought to take a stab at social appreciation as opposed to assignment, teaming up with neighborhood specialists and networks while integrating social components into crusades.

Restriction of publicizing content goes past language interpretation. It includes adjusting efforts to suit the particular necessities and inclinations of each market. This might incorporate changing visuals, adjusting informing, or consolidating socially pertinent subjects.

Confinement exhibits a pledge to drawing in with the nearby crowd based on their conditions, encouraging a feeling of association and reverberation.

Worldwide brands face the test of keeping a predictable brand picture while adjusting to different social settings. Finding some kind of harmony between a normalized worldwide brand and restricted crusades requires an insightful methodology. Center brand values and informing can stay predictable, while explicit components are customized to line up with nearby social standards. Consistency in brand pith, joined with social responsiveness, fabricates a worldwide brand that feels natural yet important in different business sectors.

Shopper trust is firmly connected to social validness. Credibility in promoting suggests a veritable comprehension and regard for the social qualities and subtleties of the interest group. Brands that show social legitimacy fabricate entrust with shoppers, cultivating long haul connections. Alternately, saw lack of care or social slips up can dissolve trust and affect brand discernment.

Social contemplations are especially urgent in the advanced domain, where missions can contact worldwide crowds momentarily. Online entertainment, specifically, gives a stage to brands to draw in with different crowds. Publicists should be receptive to social patterns, online ways of behaving, and the particular manners of every stage to amplify the effect of computerized crusades. Social listening devices can be important in figuring out shopper feeling and adjusting procedures progressively.

Powerhouse showcasing, a pervasive methodology in the computerized age, requires cautious thought of social fit. Brands joining forces with powerhouses should guarantee that the powerhouse's qualities line up with those of the brand and resound with the ideal interest group. Nearby powerhouses who are all around respected in their social setting can give a credible extension between the brand and its crowd.

Information security concerns are vital in the computerized period, and social mentalities towards protection fluctuate generally. Sponsors should explore neighborhood guidelines and buyer assumptions about information assurance. Regarding and obviously conveying protection rehearses assembles entrust with purchasers and mitigates the gamble of crossing paths with social assumptions.

Emergency the board in promoting requests a socially educated approach. Publicists should be ready to answer quickly and properly to emergencies that might emerge because of social misinterpretations or false impressions. Having an emergency correspondence plan that thinks about social subtleties and draws in with neighborhood partners is fundamental for relieving reputational harm and reestablishing trust.

Publicizing and advancement are basic parts of any business technique, assuming a vital part in building brand mindfulness, driving deals, and laying out major areas of strength for a presence. In the present dynamic and cutthroat business scene, organizations need compelling and imaginative ways of arriving at their interest group and separate themselves from contenders. This exhaustive investigation dives into the complex universe of publicizing and advancement, looking at key ideas, systems, and the developing scene of promoting correspondence.

At its center, publicizing is the workmanship and study of making powerful messages to impart a brand's incentive to the interest group. This correspondence intends to impact purchaser conduct, make brand faithfulness, and at last drive deals. Advancement, then again, envelops a more extensive range of exercises intended to invigorate interest, preliminary, or acquisition of an item or administration. Both publicizing and advancement are necessary parts of the showcasing blend, working couple to accomplish authoritative objectives.

The computerized unrest has changed the manner in which organizations approach publicizing and advancement. The approach of the web, online entertainment, and other computerized channels has extended the compass and capacities of showcasing correspondence. Web based publicizing, online entertainment showcasing, powerhouse joint efforts, and content promoting have become fundamental devices for organizations hoping to interface with their crowd in a more customized and drawing in way.

One of the basic parts of publicizing and advancement is figuring out the ideal interest group. Effective missions are based on a profound comprehension of customer needs, inclinations, and ways of behaving. Statistical surveying assumes a vital part in this cycle, giving important experiences that educate the improvement regarding powerful correspondence methodologies. By distinguishing the objective segment and fitting messages to reverberate with their inclinations and values, organizations can make more significant and applicable publicizing and advancement crusades.

The shift from customary to computerized publicizing has achieved a worldview change in the manner organizations designate their showcasing financial plans. Computerized publicizing offers a degree of accuracy and quantifiability that customary channels frequently need. With apparatuses like Google Examination, organizations can follow the presentation of online missions continuously, considering information driven direction and improvement. This information driven approach empowers organizations to refine their techniques, dispense assets all the more successfully, and amplify the profit from venture (return for money invested) from their publicizing and advancement endeavors.

Online entertainment stages have arisen as strong channels for publicizing and advancement. The capacity to target explicit socioeconomics, take part continuously discussions, and influence client produced content has made online entertainment a foundation of current promoting procedures.

Powerhouse promoting, a subset of virtual entertainment showcasing, includes teaming up with people who have a huge following and impact over their crowd. This type of advancement can upgrade brand validity and arrive at new portions of the market.

Content showcasing has likewise acquired conspicuousness as a methodology to offer some incentive to the crowd while quietly advancing items or administrations. By making applicable and significant substance, organizations can set up a good foundation for themselves as industry specialists, fabricate entrust with their crowd, and drive natural traffic to their sites. Blog entries, articles, recordings, and infographics are only a couple of instances of content showcasing drives that add to a comprehensive publicizing and advancement system.

In the domain of customary promoting, TV, radio, print, open air publicizing actually assume a part in arriving at specific socioeconomics. While computerized channels offer high level focusing on capacities, conventional media can be compelling in building expansive mindfulness and contacting crowds that may not be as carefully locked in. Coordinated crusades that influence both advanced and customary channels can boost reach and effect.

The idea of coordinated promoting correspondence (IMC) highlights the significance of keeping up with consistency across different correspondence channels. A firm and bound together message upgrades brand review and builds up key brand credits. IMC includes planning all components of the promoting blend to convey a consistent and incorporated brand insight. This approach guarantees that publicizing and advancement endeavors line up with more extensive promoting and business goals.

Brand situating is a basic thought in publicizing and advancement. How a brand is seen in the personalities of customers can essentially affect its prosperity. Powerful situating includes recognizing and conveying an interesting offer that separates the brand from contenders. Whether a brand is situated as an extravagance item, a reasonable choice, or a creative arrangement, this situating ought to be reliably reflected in all publicizing and limited time endeavors.

Inventiveness is one more sign of effective publicizing and advancement. Noteworthy and significant missions frequently come from imaginative reasoning that gets through the messiness and catches the crowd's consideration. Whether it's a cunning slogan, an outwardly striking picture, or a diverting video, innovative components can hoist a mission and make it more shareable, adding to its viral potential.

The job of information in publicizing and advancement couldn't possibly be more significant. The advanced period has introduced a time of remarkable information accessibility, permitting advertisers to accumulate experiences into purchaser conduct, inclinations, and commitment designs. Breaking down this information engages organizations to go with informed choices, refine focusing on methodologies, and customize content to improve importance.

AI calculations and man-made consciousness (computer based intelligence) further improve the abilities of information driven publicizing, empowering dynamic promotion focusing on and personalization at scale.

Personalization is a critical pattern in contemporary publicizing and advancement. Shoppers are immersed with messages everyday, and conventional, one-size-fits-all missions frequently neglect to resound. Customized publicizing tailors messages to individual inclinations, ways of behaving, and socioeconomics, making a more private association with the crowd. This can be accomplished through designated messages, modified item suggestions, and customized content in light of client information.

The moral contemplations of publicizing and advancement are progressively going under examination. As purchasers become seriously knowing and socially cognizant, organizations should explore the sensitive harmony between advancing their items and administrations and sticking to moral norms. Straightforwardness, credibility, and dependable publicizing rehearses are urgent for building entrust with customers and keeping a positive brand picture.

Powerhouse showcasing, while a strong instrument, likewise presents moral difficulties. Revelation of associations, genuineness of supports, and the likely effect on weak crowds are regions that require cautious thought. Finding some kind of harmony between utilizing powerhouses for their compass and keeping up with moral guidelines is fundamental for long haul brand validity.

Administrative structures administering publicizing and advancement shift all around the world and are likely to visit refreshes. Publicists should remain informed about important guidelines to guarantee consistence and stay away from lawful repercussions. Deluding claims, deliberate deception, and protection concerns are among the issues that can prompt administrative investigation. Adjusting to developing guidelines is a continuous obligation regarding organizations participated in publicizing and advancement.

Emergency the board is one more angle that organizations should be ready for in the domain of publicizing and advancement. In the period of online entertainment, a solitary slip up can grow into an advertising emergency that can harm a brand's standing. Opportune and straightforward correspondence, combined with a proactive way to deal with resolving issues, is fundamental for moderating the effect of emergencies and reconstructing entrust with buyers.

The estimation of publicizing and advancement viability is a complex yet pivotal part of mission the executives. Key execution pointers (KPIs, for example, reach, commitment, transformation rates, and profit from speculation give experiences into the progress of a mission. An extensive comprehension of these measurements permits organizations to enhance their methodologies, dispense assets decisively, and accomplish improved brings about ensuing efforts.

The fate of publicizing and advancement is probably going to be formed by arising innovations and moving customer ways of behaving. Increased reality (AR) and augmented reality (VR) are ready to alter the manner in which brands draw in with crowds, offering vivid and intuitive encounters. Voice search, chatbots, and man-made brainpower driven personalization are additionally expected to assume progressively critical parts in forming the fate of advertising correspondence.

As the publicizing and advancement scene keeps on developing, versatility and dexterity are becoming crucial attributes for organizations. Remaining in front of patterns, embracing new advancements, and constantly refining systems in light of customer bits of knowledge will be critical to keeping an upper hand. The crossing point of imagination, information, and innovation will drive the following flood of advancements in publicizing and advancement, reshaping the manner in which organizations associate with their crowds.

Chapter 9

Risk Management and Adaptability

Risk the board and flexibility are two essential components in exploring the intricacies of the present dynamic and always advancing business scene. In a period set apart by fast mechanical headways, international vulnerabilities, and unexpected worldwide occasions, associations must proactively recognize, survey, and alleviate dangers to guarantee their maintainability and achievement. Besides, developing versatility inside an association is fundamental for answering successfully to changes and difficulties, cultivating advancement, and keeping an upper hand.

At the core of compelling gamble the board lies the most common way of distinguishing expected dangers and weaknesses that could affect an association's goals. These dangers can appear in different structures, going from monetary and functional to key and reputational. To explore this mind boggling scene, associations utilize a methodical way to deal with distinguish, survey, and focus on gambles. The gamble the board cycle ordinarily implies risk distinguishing proof, risk evaluation, risk moderation, and progressing checking and audit.

Risk distinguishing proof is the underlying move toward the gamble the board cycle, implying the ID of potential dangers that could influence an association's objectives. This interaction requires an exhaustive assessment of interior and outside factors that might present dangers or valuable open doors. Inward factors might incorporate functional failures, asset limitations, or human blunder, while outside factors include monetary variances, administrative changes, or international occasions.

Whenever gambles are distinguished, the following stage is risk appraisal, where the probability and effect of each hazard are assessed. This includes a quantitative and subjective investigation to decide the possible outcomes and the likelihood of event. Associations frequently use risk networks or scoring frameworks to focus on gambles with in view of seriousness and probability, permitting them to zero in their assets on tending to the main dangers.

Having surveyed the dangers, associations continue on toward risk alleviation, where procedures are created to limit the effect of recognized chances. Relief methodologies can incorporate gamble aversion, risk move, risk decrease, or acknowledgment.

Evasion includes avoiding exercises that present critical dangers, while risk move implies moving the obligation regarding possible misfortunes to another party, like through protection or rethinking. Risk decrease centers around carrying out measures to diminish the probability or effect of an endlessly risk acknowledgment recognizes the gamble however picks not to make explicit moves to moderate it.

Successful gamble the executives likewise requires continuous checking and survey to guarantee that the gamble scene is constantly reevaluated considering evolving conditions. Normal updates to take a chance with evaluations and changes in accordance with moderation techniques are basic to keeping up with flexibility notwithstanding developing dangers.

In lined up with risk the board, versatility arises as a correlative and similarly fundamental hierarchical characteristic. Flexibility alludes to an association's ability to change its techniques, designs, and cycles in light of changes in its outside climate. In a quickly developing business scene, described by mechanical disturbances, market vacillations, and capricious occasions, flexibility is a critical determinant of an association's endurance and achievement.

One part of authoritative versatility is the capacity to expect and proactively answer changes in the outside climate. This includes keeping up to date with industry patterns, arising advances, and international improvements to recognize amazing open doors and dangers right off the bat. Associations that effectively check their outer climate are better situated to change their methodologies and activities fully expecting future difficulties.

In addition, versatility is firmly connected to hierarchical culture. Developing a culture that values advancement, trial and error, and nonstop learning cultivates a climate where representatives are urged to adjust to change. A versatile culture enables representatives to embrace groundbreaking thoughts, proceed with carefully thought out plans of action, and gain from disappointments, cultivating a dynamic and strong association.

The job of authority is essential in driving flexibility inside an association. Pioneers should advocate a dream for change, impart the requirement for transformation, and offer the essential help and assets for execution. An initiative style that supports open correspondence, joint effort, and adaptability adds to a culture of flexibility where workers feel engaged to unhesitatingly explore change.

With regards to gamble with the board, versatility turns out to be especially huge. While risk the executives expects to distinguish and alleviate likely dangers, the capacity to adjust guarantees that associations can answer actually to unanticipated difficulties that might not have been at first recognized. An unbending or firm association might battle to adapt to surprising disturbances, though a versatile one is better prepared to explore vulnerabilities.

The coordination of chance administration and versatility is exemplified in situation arranging, an essential device that imagines numerous future situations and assists associations with getting ready for a scope of conceivable outcomes. Situation arranging includes distinguishing key drivers of progress, creating conceivable situations, and evaluating the expected effect of every situation on the association. This interaction permits associations to foster adaptable techniques that can be changed in view of the unfurling conditions.

Moreover, mechanical headways assume a crucial part in upgrading both gamble the executives and versatility. The utilization of information investigation, man-made consciousness, and other arising advances empowers associations to accumulate and break down huge measures of information to recognize expected dangers and amazing open doors. Prescient investigation, for example, can assist associations with determining expected chances and survey the probability of different situations, upgrading their capacity to proactively oversee gambles.

Additionally, innovation works with authoritative flexibility by giving devices and stages to far off cooperation, spry task the executives, and ongoing correspondence. The digitalization of cycles empowers associations to answer quickly to changes in the business climate, adjust their tasks, and go with informed choices in view of ongoing information.

An essential part of hazard the executives and versatility is the idea of flexibility. Strength alludes to an association's capacity to endure, recuperate from, and adjust to interruptions. Building strength implies overseeing takes a chance as well as fostering the ability to return from difficulties and flourish despite misfortune.

Flexibility is developed through a blend of strong gamble the board rehearses, a versatile hierarchical culture, and the capacity to gain from encounters. Associations that view difficulties as any open doors for development and learning are better situated to fabricate strength over the long haul. Versatile associations likewise will more often than not have enhanced income streams, adaptable functional designs, serious areas of strength for and with partners, which add to their capacity to weather conditions storms and arise more grounded.

Joint effort and associations are extra aspects that add to both gamble the executives and flexibility. Participating in essential coordinated efforts with different associations, industry accomplices, and even contenders can improve an association's capacity to share bits of knowledge, assets, and best practices. Joint efforts can likewise give an aggregate reaction to broad difficulties, like administrative changes or innovative disturbances, cultivating a stronger and versatile environment.

All in all, risk the executives and flexibility are indivisible components that associations should develop to flourish in the present quick moving and unusual business climate.

Compelling gamble the board includes a precise way to deal with distinguishing, surveying, and relieving likely dangers, while versatility requires an association to change its procedures, designs, and cycles because of changes in its outer climate.

Both gamble the board and versatility are interconnected and commonly building up. An association that effectively oversees gambles is more ready to adjust to unanticipated difficulties, and a versatile association is stronger despite chances. The incorporation of these two components is fundamental for building a hearty and supportable association that can explore vulnerabilities, profit by open doors, and arise more grounded from misfortunes. As associations keep on developing in the 21st hundred years, the cooperative energy between risk the executives and versatility will assume a focal part in forming their prosperity and life span.

9.1 Identifying and mitigating risks associated with international trade

Worldwide exchange is a mind boggling and dynamic scene that offers huge open doors for organizations looking for worldwide extension. In any case, alongside the expected prizes, participating in worldwide exchange opens associations to a bunch of dangers. These dangers can go from monetary and political vulnerabilities to administrative difficulties and social contrasts. Really distinguishing and moderating these dangers is basic for organizations to explore the complexities of global exchange and guarantee supported achievement.

One of the essential difficulties in worldwide exchange is cash risk. Variances in return rates can considerably affect the expense of products, net revenues, and in general monetary execution. Associations participated in cross-line exchanges should intently screen cash developments and execute techniques to support against antagonistic swapping scale changes. Using monetary instruments, for example, forward agreements or cash choices can assist with moderating the effect of money risk, giving a degree of sureness in worldwide exchanges.

Political and administrative dangers likewise pose a potential threat in the domain of global exchange. Political unsteadiness, changes in government strategies, and administrative vulnerabilities can fundamentally influence a business' tasks and productivity. It is urgent for associations to direct careful political and administrative gamble evaluations prior to entering new business sectors. This includes figuring out the political environment, surveying the soundness of the public authority, and keeping up to date with any administrative changes that might affect exchange exercises. Laying areas of strength for out with neighborhood specialists, government authorities, and industry affiliations can support exploring the complex administrative scenes of various nations.

Exchange obstructions, including duties and amounts, address one more class of dangers that associations should fight with in global exchange. These boundaries can arise because of international strains, exchange questions, or changes in economic accords.

Exhaustive statistical surveying and a careful comprehension of economic deals and levies are fundamental for organizations to expect and answer potential exchange obstructions. Enhancing the store network and taking into account elective business sectors can give a competitive edge in relieving the effect of exchange obstructions.

Social contrasts present a one of a kind arrangement of difficulties in global exchange, enveloping varieties in language, strategic policies, and normal practices. Mistaken assumptions emerging from social contrasts can prompt correspondence breakdowns, influencing associations with clients, providers, and different partners. To moderate social dangers, associations ought to put resources into social preparation for their faculty and draw in neighborhood specialists who can give experiences into the subtleties of leading business in unambiguous areas. Building solid diverse relational abilities inside the labor force can improve coordinated effort and encourage positive connections in global business sectors.

Production network weaknesses represent a huge gamble in worldwide exchange, particularly in a globalized economy where interconnected supply chains are the standard. Interruptions because of catastrophic events, international occasions, or unexpected emergencies can upset the progression of merchandise and effect creation plans. Carrying out powerful store network the board works on, including risk planning, expansion of providers, and the utilization of innovation for continuous checking, can improve flexibility and alleviate the effect of production network interruptions.

Consistence with global exchange regulations and guidelines is central for associations participated in cross-line exercises. Rebelliousness can bring about legitimate results, fines, and harm to the association's standing. Remaining informed about exchange regulations, trade controls, and endorses pertinent to explicit business sectors is essential. Laying out a hearty consistence program that incorporates ordinary preparation, reviews, and observing guarantees that the association works inside the legitimate system of global exchange.

Licensed innovation (IP) chances are likewise a worry in global exchange, especially in business sectors where IP security might be more vulnerable. Unapproved use or encroachment of protected innovation, including licenses, brand names, and copyrights, can prompt monetary misfortunes and disintegrate an organization's upper hand. Directing careful reasonable level of effort on the IP scene in target showcases and executing measures, for example, enrolling brand names and licenses can assist with safeguarding protected innovation resources in the worldwide field.

One more critical gamble in worldwide exchange is the potential for moral and social obligation issues. Participating in business exercises in various nations expects associations to stick to assorted moral principles and accepted practices. Issues connected with work rehearses, ecological effect, and corporate social obligation can become wellsprings of reputational risk on the off chance that not oversaw successfully.

Embracing straightforward and moral strategic policies, leading normal reviews, and effectively captivating with partners can add to a positive corporate picture and relieve the gamble of reputational harm.

The worldwide idea of global exchange presents network safety gambles with that associations should address to safeguard delicate information and keep up with the honesty of their activities. The expanded dependence on computerized advances and online stages for exchange exchanges conveys organizations defenseless against digital intimidations, for example, information breaks, ransomware assaults, and protected innovation robbery. Carrying out hearty network protection measures, including encryption, firewalls, and representative preparation on network protection best practices, is fundamental for defending data in the interconnected universe of worldwide exchange.

Natural and supportability chances are acquiring noticeable quality with regards to global exchange as partners progressively focus on earth mindful strategic policies. Associations need to evaluate the natural effect of their activities, supply chains, and items. Inability to address natural dangers can bring about administrative rebelliousness, harm to mark notoriety, and the deficiency of piece of the pie. Embracing economical strategic approaches, getting applicable certificates, and straightforwardly conveying natural endeavors to partners can help relieve ecological and supportability gambles in global exchange.

The intricacy of worldwide exchange requires an extensive and coordinated way to deal with risk the executives. A gamble the board structure custom-made to the subtleties of worldwide exchange ought to incorporate gamble ID, evaluation, moderation, and ceaseless observing. This proactive methodology empowers associations to expect likely dangers, foster procedures to alleviate them, and adjust to changing conditions in the worldwide commercial center.

Participating in careful gamble ID implies directing extensive gamble evaluations well defined for each market or district wherein a business works. This incorporates assessing political, financial, social, mechanical, legitimate, and natural factors that might influence global exchange exercises. Teaming up with neighborhood specialists, industry affiliations, and government offices can give important experiences into locale explicit dangers and administrative necessities.

Risk evaluation in worldwide exchange requires a nuanced comprehension of the interconnectedness of dangers and their true capacity flowing impacts. Surveying the interdependencies between various kinds of dangers, for example, political and production network gambles, empowers associations to foster all encompassing gamble relief techniques. Quantitative strategies, like situation examination and demonstrating, can help with evaluating the expected monetary effect of different dangers and illuminate independent direction.

Moderating dangers in worldwide exchange implies the turn of events and execution of custom-made risk the board methodologies. Cash risk, for instance, can be relieved using monetary instruments like forward agreements or money choices. Political dangers might be overseen by differentiating activities across politically stable business sectors, getting political gamble protection, or laying out alternate courses of action for expected disturbances.

Inventory network dangers can be moderated by expanding providers, carrying out repetitive store network structures, and utilizing cutting edge innovations for ongoing checking. Consistence gambles require the foundation of vigorous consistence programs, including normal preparation for representatives, intensive reasonable level of investment on exchanging accomplices, and constant observing of administrative changes.

Social dangers, then again, can be moderated through social preparation programs, the work of nearby staff with social mastery, and the improvement of an adaptable correspondence methodology that obliges social subtleties. Moral and social obligation gambles expect associations to embrace straightforward and moral strategic policies, direct customary reviews, and draw in with partners to comprehend and address cultural assumptions.

Nonstop observing is a vital part of successful gamble the board in worldwide exchange. The worldwide business climate is dynamic, and dangers can develop quickly. Associations should lay out components for ongoing checking of important markers, like international turns of events, financial patterns, and administrative changes. This empowers organizations to adjust their techniques expeditiously in light of arising dangers and open doors.

Besides, associations took part in global exchange ought to encourage a culture of chance mindfulness and responsiveness at all levels of the association. This includes instructing workers about the significance of chance administration, giving preparation on risk recognizable proof and relief systems, and empowering .

9.2 Strategies for adapting to changing market conditions

Exploring difficulties is an inborn piece of the business scene, and a few organizations stand apart for their versatility, flexibility, and vital dynamic despite difficulty. Inspecting the encounters of these organizations gives important bits of knowledge into compelling systems for beating difficulties and making long haul progress.

One prominent model is Apple Inc., an organization that has reliably shown its capacity to explore difficulties and keep serious areas of strength for a position. Apple confronted a huge test in the last part of the 1990s when it was wrestling with monetary misfortunes, a declining piece of the pie, and struggles under the surface. In 1997, Mac's fellow benefactor, Steve Occupations, got back to the organization, and under his initiative, Macintosh went through a striking change.

Occupations executed a progression of vital drives, including smoothing out the product offering, presenting imaginative and tastefully satisfying plans, and zeroing in on the client experience. The presentation of notorious items like the iMac, iPod, iPhone, and iPad exhibited Macintosh's obligation to advancement and client driven plan. These items re-imagined their individual business sectors as well as added to Apple's resurgence as a worldwide innovation pioneer.

Apple's prosperity can be credited to its accentuation on making a consistent biological system of equipment, programming, and administrations, encouraging client faithfulness. The organization's capacity to expect and shape purchaser inclinations, combined with a persevering spotlight on quality and configuration, empowered it to conquer difficulties and set up a good foundation for itself as quite possibly of the most important and powerful organization on the planet.

Another illustrative case is that of Netflix, an organization that reformed media outlets by moving from a customary DVD rental model to a membership based web-based feature. In the mid 2000s, while streaming innovation was still in its outset, Netflix confronted difficulties as contest from customary link suppliers and the declining pertinence of actual media.

To adjust to changing economic situations, Netflix decisively put resources into content creation and progressed to a streaming-first model. The organization's accentuation on unique programming, for example, "Place of Cards" and "More interesting Things," separated it from contenders as well as drawn in a developing supporter base. The adaptability of the streaming stage permitted Netflix to adjust to advancing buyer ways of behaving, for example, marathon watching and on-request satisfied utilization.

In addition, Netflix's worldwide extension further epitomizes its flexibility. The organization perceived the capability of the worldwide market and forcefully extended its administrations universally, beating difficulties connected with content authorizing, social contrasts, and shifting web frameworks. Today, Netflix is a predominant power in the worldwide streaming industry, showing the way that essential variation can transform difficulties into open doors.

In the auto area, Tesla Inc. stands apart as an organization that effectively explored difficulties to reclassify the business. Established by Elon Musk, Tesla confronted doubt and incredulity from customary automakers and financial backers. Musk's vision was to speed up the world's change to economical energy, however accomplishing this objective required conquering various obstacles.

Tesla confronted monetary difficulties, creation misfortunes, and questions about the reasonability of electric vehicles. Nonetheless, the organization endured in its obligation to advancement, persistently refining its electric vehicle innovation and energy items. The send off of the Model S, trailed by the Model 3, exhibited Tesla's capacity to deliver elite execution electric vehicles at scale.

Furthermore, Tesla's emphasis on vertical coordination, including fabricating its batteries and creating self-driving innovation, situated it as a forerunner in the electric vehicle market. The organization's market capitalization took off, unparalleled that of customary automakers, flagging a change in outlook in the business. Tesla's prosperity features the significance of visionary authority, mechanical development, and a pledge to manageability in defeating difficulties.

The drug business offers a model in Novartis, a global drug organization that effectively explored difficulties through essential changes. In the mid 2000s, Novartis confronted patent terminations, conventional contest, and a need to adjust to changing medical services elements. Under the initiative of Chief Daniel Vasella, the organization sought after a progression of vital moves to revive its portfolio.

Novartis stripped non-center organizations, procured designated resources, and put resources into innovative work to construct a strong pipeline of imaginative medications. The obtaining of biotechnology organization Chiron and the improvement of advanced drugs, like Gleevec for leukemia and Gilenya for different sclerosis, added to Novartis' prosperity.

Besides, Novartis embraced a differentiated plan of action, growing past drugs to incorporate divisions zeroed in on generics, immunizations, and shopper wellbeing. This enhancement gave flexibility against market vacillations and situated Novartis as a far reaching medical organization. The capacity to adjust to changing economic situations while keeping an emphasis on development and enhancement added to Novartis' proceeded with progress in the drug business.

The retail area presents a model in Amazon, an organization that changed online business and changed into a worldwide innovation and retail goliath. Established by Jeff Bezos during the 1990s, Amazon at first confronted doubt about the practicality of online retail. Be that as it may, Bezos' drawn out vision and obligation to consumer loyalty drove Amazon's persevering spotlight on proficiency, comfort, and advancement.

Amazon explored difficulties, for example, the website bubble burst, developing buyer inclinations, and serious rivalry. The organization enhanced its contributions past books to turn into a one-stop online commercial center for an immense range of items. The presentation of Amazon Prime with its quick delivery and selective substance further upgraded the client experience.

Furthermore, Amazon embraced innovation as a center part of its system. The improvement of Amazon Web Administrations (AWS), the organization's distributed computing stage, gave another income stream as well as turned into a basic framework part for organizations around the world. The procurement of Entire Food sources in 2017 denoted Amazon's entrance into physical retail, displaying its flexibility and readiness to investigate new roads.

Amazon's prosperity highlights the significance of client centricity, mechanical development, and a readiness to disturb customary plans of action. The organization's capacity to adjust to changing economic situations has situated it as a prevailing power in worldwide online business and innovation.

In the domain of quick style, Zara, a lead brand of the Inditex bunch, is perceived for its extraordinary plan of action and versatility. Zara confronted difficulties intrinsic in the design business, including quickly changing customer patterns, extreme contest, and the customary occasional model of dress creation. Be that as it may, Zara's way to deal with design retailing put it aside.

Zara's key procedure spins around quick moving, in an upward direction coordinated store network the board. The organization limited creation lead times, empowering it to rapidly answer arising style. Zara's spry production network permitted it to acquaint new plans with stores in practically no time, an unmistakable difference to the conventional design industry's occasional cycles. This procedure diminished the gamble of stock out of date quality as well as made a feeling of shortage and desperation among buyers.

Besides, Zara embraced innovation in its production network and stock administration frameworks. The utilization of information examination and constant deals data informed choices on creation and restocking, guaranteeing that stores were loaded with the most popular things. Zara's plan of action represents the significance of readiness, information driven direction, and vertical mix in adjusting to the high speed nature of the design business.

The energy area offers a model in NextEra Energy, a main clean energy organization that effectively explored moves in the progress to sustainable power. NextEra confronted the test of adjusting to a changing energy scene set apart by the shift towards manageability, expanded administrative investigation, and the requirement for cleaner energy sources.

Under the initiative of Chief Jim Robo, NextEra decisively situated itself as a forerunner in sustainable power, with an emphasis on wind, sunlight based, and battery capacity. The organization put vigorously in sustainable power projects, exploiting tax breaks and progressions in sustainable advancements. The securing of Florida Power and Light Organization fortified NextEra's situation in the utility area and worked with the extension of its sustainable power portfolio.

Besides, NextEra Energy embraced development and mechanical progressions in energy capacity. The improvement of huge scope battery capacity projects tended to the discontinuous idea of sustainable power sources, adding to lattice soundness and unwavering quality. NextEra's prosperity represents the significance of vital prescience, a guarantee to maintainability, and utilizing mechanical progressions in exploring difficulties in the energy area.

In the monetary administrations area, JPMorgan Pursue embodies an organization that successfully explored difficulties, especially during times of financial vulnerability. The worldwide monetary emergency of 2008 introduced a critical test for the financial business, and JPMorgan Pursue, under the initiative of President Jamie Dimon, arose as perhaps of the strongest foundation.

JPMorgan Pursue decisively dealt with its gamble openness, fortified its accounting report, and explored through the intricacies of the monetary emergency more successfully than a considerable lot of its friends. The procurement of Bear Stearns and

Washington Shared situated JPMorgan Pursue as a central participant in the business. Dimon's accentuation on risk the executives, an expanded plan of action, and an emphasis on client connections added to the bank's versatility.

Also, JPMorgan Pursue showed versatility in answering changing administrative scenes. The execution of upgraded risk the board rehearses, consistence measures, and a promise to straightforwardness situated the bank as a forerunner in exploring administrative difficulties. JPMorgan Pursue's capacity to adjust to monetary vulnerabilities and administrative changes highlights the significance of compelling gamble the executives and key versatility in the monetary administrations area.

In the innovation area, Microsoft's change under the administration of Satya Nadella fills in as an important illustration of effectively exploring difficulties. In the mid 2000s, Microsoft confronted difficulties connected with the decay of its strength in the PC market, contest from arising advances, and a requirement for social change.

Satya Nadella, named as Chief in 2014, started a social shift inside Microsoft, encouraging a more cooperative and creative climate. He underlined a "cloud-first, portable first" methodology, zeroing in on distributed computing and extending Microsoft's presence in programming and administrations. The obtaining of LinkedIn and GitHub further supplemented Microsoft's vision of enabling people and associations.

Nadella's essential course revived Microsoft's pertinence in the innovation business. The progress of cloud-based administrations, like Sky blue, and the membership based model of Microsoft 365 added to the organization's monetary development. Microsoft's capacity to adjust to the advancing innovation scene and embrace new plans of action epitomizes the significance of visionary administration and key dexterity.

These models feature that fruitful route of difficulties includes a blend of vital prescience, flexibility, development, and a client driven approach. Organizations that have really defeated snags have frequently embraced change, utilized innovation, and exhibited a guarantee to ceaseless improvement. The capacity to expect and answer developing economic situations is a sign of persevering through outcome in the powerful universe of business.

9.3 Highlighting companies that successfully navigated challenges

Fruitful route of provokes is a demonstration of the flexibility, key intuition, and versatility of organizations across different ventures. Looking at these organizations gives significant experiences into the assorted methodologies and systems utilized to defeat impediments and arise more grounded even with misfortune.

Apple Inc.: Spearheading Advancement and Plan

One of the most notorious examples of overcoming adversity in the innovation business is Apple Inc. Established by Steve Occupations, Steve Wozniak, and Ronald Wayne in 1976, Mac confronted a huge decline during the 1990s. The organization wrestled with monetary misfortunes, declining portion of the overall industry, and unseen struggles. Be that as it may, the arrival of Steve Occupations in 1997 denoted a defining moment for Macintosh.

Under Positions' visionary initiative, Apple went through an essential change that zeroed in on development and client driven plan. Occupations smoothed out the product offering, presenting notorious items like the iMac, iPod, iPhone, and iPad. These gadgets upset their separate business sectors as well as exhibited Apple's obligation to smooth plan and client experience.

Apple's prosperity can be ascribed to its capacity to expect and shape customer inclinations. By making a consistent environment of equipment, programming, and administrations, Apple developed client devotion and kept areas of strength for a position. The organization's versatility, combined with a persistent spotlight on quality and configuration, has empowered it to explore difficulties and set up a good foundation for itself as a worldwide innovation pioneer.

Netflix: Gushing to Progress

Netflix, a disruptor in media outlets, changed from a DVD rental support of a worldwide streaming monster. In the mid 2000s, Netflix confronted difficulties like contest from conventional link suppliers and the lessening significance of actual media. Notwithstanding, the organization decisively put resources into content creation and progressed to a streaming-first model.

The presentation of unique programming, including acclaimed series like "Place of Cards" and "More bizarre Things," put Netflix aside from contenders. The organization's obligation to on-request happy utilization and marathon watching ways of behaving resounded with purchasers. Besides, Netflix's forceful worldwide development defeated difficulties connected with content permitting, social contrasts, and changing web foundations.

By adjusting to changing customer ways of behaving and utilizing innovation, Netflix turned into a predominant power in the worldwide streaming industry.

The organization's prosperity shows the significance of vital substance speculations, an emphasis on client experience, and a worldwide development methodology in exploring difficulties and remaining ahead in a powerful market.

Tesla Inc.: Upsetting the Car Business

Tesla Inc., drove by visionary business person Elon Musk, has reclassified the car business through its attention on electric vehicles (EVs) and practical energy arrangements. Tesla confronted wariness and difficulties, including monetary imperatives, creation mishaps, and questions about the practicality of EVs. Nonetheless, the organization's obligation to advancement and maintainability has pushed it to progress.

Tesla decisively situated itself as a forerunner in the EV market by persistently refining its innovation and growing its product offering. The presentation of elite execution electric vehicles like the Model S and the more reasonable Model 3 collected far reaching praise. Tesla's accentuation on vertical reconciliation, including producing its batteries and creating self-driving innovation, further hardened its situation on the lookout.

The organization's market capitalization outperformed conventional automakers, flagging a change in outlook in the business. Tesla's prosperity highlights the significance of visionary authority, mechanical development, and a pledge to manageability in exploring difficulties and reshaping whole enterprises.

Novartis: Enhancing in Drugs

Novartis, a global drug organization, effectively explored difficulties in the profoundly cutthroat drug industry. In the mid 2000s, the organization confronted patent terminations, nonexclusive contest, and the need to adjust to changing medical care elements. Under the administration of President Daniel Vasella, Novartis sought after essential moves to rejuvenate its portfolio.

Novartis carried out a progression of vital drives, including stripping non-center organizations, getting designated resources, and putting resources into innovative work. The securing of biotechnology organization Chiron and the improvement of cutting edge drugs, like Gleevec for leukemia and Gilenya for various sclerosis, added to Novartis' prosperity.

The organization embraced a differentiated plan of action by growing past drugs to incorporate divisions zeroed in on generics, immunizations, and shopper wellbeing. This enhancement gave strength against market variances and situated Novartis as a far reaching medical organization. Novartis' capacity to adjust to changing economic situations while keeping an emphasis on development and expansion added to its proceeded with progress in the drug business.

Amazon: Reclassifying Online business and Innovation

Amazon, established by Jeff Bezos in 1994, is a groundbreaking example of overcoming adversity in the web based business and innovation areas.

At first an internet based book shop, Amazon confronted doubt about the reasonability of online retail. Be that as it may, Jeff Bezos' drawn out vision and client driven approach drove Amazon's constant spotlight on proficiency, accommodation, and development.

Amazon decisively differentiated its contributions past books to turn into a one-stop online commercial center for a huge swath of items. The presentation of Amazon Prime, with its quick delivery and selective substance, further improved the client experience. Amazon's hug of innovation as a center part of its methodology, including the improvement of Amazon Web Administrations (AWS), situated it as a forerunner in both online business and distributed computing.

The obtaining of Entire Food varieties denoted Amazon's entrance into physical retail, exhibiting its versatility and eagerness to investigate new roads. Amazon's prosperity highlights the significance of client centricity, mechanical development, and an eagerness to disturb customary plans of action in exploring difficulties and remaining ahead in the quickly advancing universe of retail and innovation.

Zara: Quick Style and Spry Stockpile Chains

Zara, a leader brand of the Inditex bunch, hangs out in the style business for its novel plan of action and versatility. Zara confronted difficulties inborn in the style business, including quickly changing customer patterns, extreme rivalry, and the customary occasional model of attire creation. Notwithstanding, Zara's way to deal with design retailing put it aside.

Zara's key procedure spins around speedy, in an upward direction coordinated production network the executives. The organization limited creation lead times, empowering it to rapidly answer arising style. This coordinated production network permitted Zara to acquaint new plans with stores in practically no time, an unmistakable difference to the customary style industry's occasional cycles.

Zara's accentuation on information driven direction and vertical joining, joined with its utilization of innovation in production network and stock administration, embodies the significance of deftness and versatility in the quick moving universe of style retail. The organization's prosperity lies in its capacity to remain in front of patterns, decrease time-to-showcase, and make a need to keep moving among purchasers.

NextEra Energy: Driving the Spotless Energy Progress

NextEra Energy, a main clean energy organization, has effectively explored provokes in the progress to environmentally friendly power. The organization confronted the need to adjust to a changing energy scene set apart by maintainability objectives, expanded administrative examination, and a shift towards cleaner energy sources.

Under the administration of President Jim Robo, NextEra decisively situated itself as a forerunner in environmentally friendly power, with an emphasis on wind, sun based, and battery capacity. The organization put vigorously in environmentally friendly power projects, exploiting tax breaks and progressions in sustainable advances. The procurement of Florida Power and Light Organization reinforced NextEra's situation in the utility area and worked with the extension of its environmentally friendly power portfolio.

NextEra Energy embraced development and mechanical progressions in energy capacity, tending to the irregular idea of sustainable power sources. The organization's prosperity delineates the significance of vital foreknowledge, a guarantee to manageability, and utilizing mechanical headways in exploring difficulties in the energy area.

JPMorgan Pursue: Versatility in Monetary Administrations

In the monetary administrations area, JPMorgan Pursue stands apart as an organization that really explored difficulties, especially during times of financial vulnerability. The worldwide monetary emergency of 2008 introduced a huge test for the financial business, and JPMorgan Pursue, under the initiative of Chief Jamie Dimon, arose as perhaps of the strongest foundation.

JPMorgan Pursue decisively dealt with its gamble openness, fortified its asset report, and explored through the intricacies of the monetary emergency more actually than a significant number of its companions. The obtaining of Bear Stearns and Washington

Shared situated JPMorgan Pursue as a vital participant in the business. Dimon's accentuation on risk the executives, an enhanced plan of action, and an emphasis on client connections added to the bank's strength.

Also, JPMorgan Pursue showed versatility in answering changing administrative scenes. The execution of upgraded risk the board rehearses, consistence measures, and a promise to straightforwardness situated the bank as a forerunner in exploring administrative difficulties. JPMorgan Pursue's capacity to adjust to monetary vulnerabilities and administrative changes highlights the significance of compelling gamble the executives and vital flexibility in the monetary administrations area.

Microsoft: Extraordinary Authority in Innovation

Microsoft's change under the administration of Satya Nadella fills in as a critical illustration of effectively exploring difficulties in the innovation area. In the mid 2000s, Microsoft confronted difficulties connected with the decay of its strength in the PC market, contest from arising innovations, and a requirement for social change.

Satya Nadella, named as Chief in 2014, started a social shift inside Microsoft, encouraging a more cooperative and creative climate.

He underlined a "cloud-first, versatile first" methodology, zeroing in on distributed computing and extending Microsoft's presence in programming and administrations. The obtaining of LinkedIn and GitHub further supplemented Microsoft's vision of enabling people and associations.

Nadella's essential course rejuvenated Microsoft's importance in the innovation business. The outcome of cloud-based administrations, like Purplish blue, and the membership based model of Microsoft 365 added to the organization's monetary development. Microsoft's capacity to adjust to the developing innovation scene and embrace new plans of action epitomizes the significance of visionary administration and key dexterity.

Printed in the USA
CPSIA information can be obtained
at www.ICGtesting.com
LVHW021417271223
767436LV00082B/2876

9 788196 809836